Getting Past the Publishing Gatekeepers is a treasure trove of suggestions for authors on what to do and what not to do with that finished manuscript, and eventually, the finished book.

— Patricia Bradley, author of the Natchez Trace Park Rangers series

A valuable resource for new and seasoned writers alike, *Getting Past the Publishing Gatekeepers* explores key elements for understanding the publishing industry by providing insights into the various aspects of breaking into publication. The book delves into ways authors can get a foot in the door and win the hearts of agents, editors, publishers, and readers. So much good information. A must read for authors!

— Cynthia Roemer, award-winning author of *Under Moonlit Skies* and *Beyond These War-Torn Lands*

I loved it. It is filled with so much good information—for the beginner and those with many books in print. And also encouragement. That alone is worth the read.

— Linda K. Rodante, author of *Warrior*

Want to position yourself to break through the barriers you face in the game of publishing? Then, *Getting Past the Publishing Gatekeepers* is the honest, heart-to-heart you never knew you needed. Chapter 35 by super reader Carrie Schmidt gets right to the core of the matter, so be sure to read that chapter as many times as you need to fuel your writing journey going forward. It's gold.

— Melony Teague, co-author of *As the Ink Flows, Devotions for Writers & Speakers*

For any aspiring author, this book is pure gold! Sharing nuggets of wisdom as well as rich insights from behind the industry curtain, these four gatekeepers provide foundational truths about what it takes to succeed and (hopefully) get published. Written with honesty and clarity, their advice offers you the opportunity to move from the slush pile to readers' hearts and from a wanna-be writer to a beloved author. A must-have resource you can't afford not to read!

— Liana George, author of the Hopeful Heart Series (*Perfectly Arranged, Perfectly Placed,* and *Perfectly Matched*) Co-founder/Creative Director at The Author's Write Hand

Clearly written with a fresh, friendly encouraging manner, *Getting Past the Publishing Gatekeepers* is an important read for authors to take to heart.

— Carrie Stuart Parks, award-winning fine artist, internationally known forensic artist, and award-winning author of the *Gwen Marcey* series

Seasoned and aspiring authors alike will appreciate these direct, simple answers to "who does what?" in the publishing industry. Myths, truths, and practical definitions are offered up in a conversational tone that paves a clear path for next steps, no matter where an author is in the writing/publishing process. A must-have for writers, written by people who know the industry inside out.

— Susan Miura, author, speaker, editor

If you're a writer or aspiring writer with questions about the gatekeepers in the industry (agents, publishers, editors, and reviewers), this book is for you. Hope Bolinger and her team have created an excellent resource that showcases the ways, the wishes, and the wisdom of these gatekeepers and what it takes to win them over. Written in an easy-to-understand way, not only is it filled with valuable tips, tidbits, and takeaways, it's also relatable, honest, and extremely helpful. Even if you've been writing for years, I guarantee you'll learn something new. I did. I wish I could have had access to this book many years ago.

— Twila Belk, writer, conference speaker, editor

Getting Past the Publishing Gatekeepers offers truly helpful advice on how to find and connect with potential readers in an easy-to-follow format.

— Beth Carpenter, author of the Northern Lights series

After years of producing a highly respected blog introducing many authors and books to the public, Carrie Schmidt has written part of an important title I wish I'd owned when I began my author/publication journey. Her chapters in *Getting Past the Publishing Gatekeepers* discussing, "How Can Authors Find New-To-Them Readers? (and keep them)" gives vital information I wish I'd known years ago. Delivered in her winsome, conversational style, it's as if your best marketing friend shares proven keys for success. This is the book we've all been waiting for. Thankfully it's here in time to benefit all of us involved in the writing/authorship industry.

— Delores Topliff, B.A., M.A., C.Ed.D., author of *Wilderness Wife*

I've known Carrie Schmidt for many years, but I'm amazed how I never stop learning from her. This book was no exception. Her chapters were brimming with practical advice on not only finding new readers, but how authors can authentically engage with them. She also shared behind-the-scenes insight into influencers, bloggers and bookstagrammers. I highly recommend this book for all authors. You'll walk away with great insight and newfound appreciation for readers who put their hearts behind our books.

— Dani Pettrey, award-winning author of the *Coastal Guardians* series

What author hasn't wondered how to reach readers? Carrie Schmidt speaks to writers–not only the successful and accomplished author, but the introverted and overwhelmed author–giving them tools to engage readers in authentic and personal ways. From tips on participating in a successful blog tour to finding and retaining enthusiastic readers, Carrie gives the author the tools they need to reach those most important of all people–the readers they long to share their stories with. You will be putting this book on your "keeper shelf" and referring to it often!

— Jan Drexler, award-winning author of *The Sign of the Calico Quartz*

Authors, you need this! Carrie delivers valuable advice on publishing, marketing, influencers, and the keys to an online presence with wit, wisdom, and a behind-the-scenes-peek into the minds of our most dedicated readers. With practical tips and useful takeaways, each chapter packs a punch. A survival guide no author should miss.

— Stephenia H. McGee, award-winning author of *The Secrets of Emberwild*

When you're a writer who wants to be a published author, the industry can look like an impenetrable fortress:

• You can't get a publisher without an agent.

• You can't get an agent without an incredibly strong platform.

• Without a published book, it's hard to attract and retain enough avid readers/reviewers to your platform.

• You don't have the money to pay an editor to help you hone your work.

With keen insights from knowledgeable and experienced industry insiders, this book demystifies the "fortress." Publishing gatekeepers are not your enemies or obstacles in your path; they're your potential allies in achieving success as an author. To get them on your side, you need to know what makes them tick. This book tells you.

— Chris Bolinger, author, *Daily Strength for Men* and *52 Weeks of Strength for Men*

Carrie Schmidt has turned a lifetime of experience championing authors into priceless tips for finding, engaging, and keeping readers. Within these chapters are practical, highlightable nuggets of wisdom for writers at any stage of their career. With an optimistic tone and encouraging heart, this guide will make a perfect addition to your bag of author tools—one you'll find yourself grabbing from first draft to release day and beyond.

— Teresa Tysinger, author of the *Laurel Cove Romance Series*

Who does more to nurture the author-reader connection than Carrie Schmidt? And now, our favorite book blogger, reviewer, and publicist is handing us her key to the gate that separates us from readers. With honesty and generosity, Carrie examines the nuances of the author-reader relationship, reveals mistakes that keep us locked on the other side, and shares expert insights so we can build a lasting relationship with readers that goes beyond selling books. Take the key. Open the gate.

— Karen Sargent, author of *Waiting for Butterflies*

As an author it's so hard to know how to connect with readers. Carrie Schmidt of *Reading Is My SuperPower* gives some insightful advice. There are suggestions that can help the novice writer as well as the multi-published author. Be prepared to take notes!

— Toni Shiloh, author of *In Search of a Prince*

Carrie Schmidt is someone I've learned knows more about Christian fiction and how to promote it, than anyone I've ever known ... certainly more than me. For Carrie to gather her knowledge together in one place and share it with the world is a true gift. I can't wait to get my hands on this book and keep it close.

— Mary Connealy, author of *The Lumber Baron's Daughters* series

Carrie Schmidt offers a veritable treasure trove of insight and information that serves as a bridge between authors and the world of book influencers. Because of Carrie's genuine warmth of spirit, brilliant mind, and breadth of experience, you'll feel like you've just sat down and had coffee with a best friend who also happens to be a genius about all-things-influencing, from how to engage in social media in a healthy, relationship-building way, to how and where to connect with readers who adore books and might just be waiting to discover yours too. If you've ever looked at the vast landscape of the book world and wondered, "how can my story find its way to the readers it was written for?"—this book holds practical, do-able, and exciting steps to make it not only possible, but enjoyable. And might I add ... chapter 35 should be required reading for every writer. Bring a tissue, and come away with a very full heart .

— Amanda Dykes, author of novels including *All the Lost Places*, *Yours is the Night*, *Set the Stars Alight*, and *Whose Waves These Are*, the 2020 Christy Award Book of the Year

If you've labored under the false assumption that once your book is written, "they" will come, *Getting Past the Publishing Gatekeepers: Winning the Hearts of Agents, Publishers, Editors, and Readers* will kindly, yet effectively, disabuse you.

If, like me, you've remained clueless as to the power of email in today's publishing arena, here's your opportunity to learn about perhaps the most effective marketing tool to date.

If you are looking for a clearly written, experience-backed summation of the too-often painful process of becoming a published author, *Gatekeepers* is your book.

Linda Fulkerson, owner of Scrivenings Press, identifies with the talented hardworking unpublished author because she has been one. But she does much more than empathize and commiserate. She moves the aspiring author from the quicksand of impossibility to the likelihood of becoming published by laying out, in a step-by-step manner, how to become a reputably published author—all the while uniquely (for those of us who aren't always able to reach to the top shelf) placing three succinct takeaways at the bottom of each chapter.

From the correct way to format a paragraph, to the importance of platform visibility, to the immutable standard of good writing, Fulkerson offers the unpublished a to-the-point guide of how to steal a publisher's heart and hold on to it.

My regret is that I didn't have a resource of this caliber lying next to my computer twenty years past.

— Jacqueline F. Wheelock, author of *God, Send Sunday*

Getting Past the Publishing GATEKEEPERS

Winning the Hearts of Agents, Publishers, Editors, and Readers

Foreword by Jane Rubietta

To Amper, Looking forward to publishing one with you! Rowena Kuo

HOPE BOLINGER
LINDA FULKERSON
ROWENA KUO
CARRIE SCHMIDT

Scrivenings PRESS
Quench your thirst for story.
www.ScriveningsPress.com

Copyright © 2022 Hope Bolinger, Linda Fulkerson, Rowena Kuo, and Carrie Schmidt

Published by Scrivenings Press LLC
15 Lucky Lane
Morrilton, Arkansas 72110
https://ScriveningsPress.com

Printed in the United States of America

All rights reserved. No part of this publication may be reproduced, stored in a retrieval system, or transmitted in any form or by any means—for example, electronic, photocopy and recording— without the prior written permission of the publisher. The only exception is brief quotation in printed reviews.

Paperback ISBN 978-1-64917-242-6

Hardcover ISBN 978-1-64917-243-3

eBook ISBN 978-1-64917-244-0

Audiobook ISBN 978-1-64917-245-7

Library of Congress Control Number: 2022945545

Cover design by Linda Fulkerson

from Hope:
To the agents, editors, publishers, and reviewers who have helped me navigate this industry.

from Linda:
To my husband Don, whose unending patience allows me to do what I do. Every kite needs a string. Thanks for hanging on all these years!

from Rowena:
For my dad, Domingo "Dominick" Gualberto, who gave me his old typewriter and taught me how to use it.
12/17/1933—08/14/2016

from Carrie:
To my Dad, my first hero and my standard for Gandalf. You would have loved this. I miss you.
1952-2021

Contents

Foreword	xvii
Introduction	xxi

Part One
Winning the Hearts of Agents
By Hope Bolinger

1. Introduction to Winning the Hearts of Agents	3
2. Let's Talk about What Agents Do	5
3. Let's Talk about Querying Agents	11
4. Let's Talk about "The Call"	21
5. Let's Talk about the Agency Contract	29
6. Let's Talk about Expectations (On Both Sides)	35
7. Let's Talk about Communications with Your Agent	45
8. Let's Talk about Submissions Strategies	51
9. Let's Talk about Leaving an Agent	57

Part Two
Winning the Hearts of Publishers
By Linda Fulkerson

10. Introduction to Winning the Hearts of Publishers	65
11. Understanding the Various Types of Publishers	69
12. Understanding What Publishers Want	77
13. Understanding What Publishers Do (And Don't Do)	83
14. Understand that Publishing is a Business	89
15. Understanding the Acquisitions Process	93
16. Understand the Publishing Process	103
17. Understand the Basics of Book Marketing	111
18. Understand the Responsibilities of an Author	121
19. Understand How to Connect with Publishers	127
20. Understand How to Beat the Odds	131

Part Three
Winning the Hearts of Editors
By Rowena Kuo

21. Introduction to Winning the Hearts of Editors	137
22. The Acquisitions Editor	141
23. When Can You Stand Your Ground on Edits?	149
24. The Developmental or Content Editor	155
25. The Line or Copy Editor	169
26. Conclusion	177

Part Four
Winning the Hearts of Readers
By Carrie Schmidt

27. Introduction to Winning the Hearts of Readers	183
28. Let's Clear the Air	189
29. The Care and Feeding of Influencers	195
30. What Makes Readers Try a New-To-Them Author?	201
31. How To Make a Good First Impression on Readers	207
32. How Do You Successfully Use Word-Of-Mouth?	215
33. Mostly Painless and Organic Reader Engagement	221
34. What Turns a Reader Off an Author?	227
35. Why Your Story Matters	233
Glossary of Terms	237
Acknowledgments	257
About Hope Bolinger	261
About Linda Fulkerson	263
About Rowena Kuo	265
About Carrie Schmidt	267
Get Free Stuff!	269
Index	271

Foreword
By Jane Rubietta

An unmentionable number of years ago, my cousin and I perched just inside the stubborn gate. How many times did I call out, "Shut the gate, please"? Or haul from my poolside chair, keeping a constant stare on my children splashing in the pool, and close the recalcitrant metal-hinged barrier? Beyond that gate roared the waves of the Atlantic Ocean, which no child should experience alone. Seriously, being a gatekeeper could be a life-or-death matter.

That day at the beach, I'd returned from my second writers' conference, and hadn't yet won the award for the most rejection letters in a room filled with several hundred writers. That award felt like an honor, because it meant that this writer-wanna-be submitted again and again.

Now, after publishing twenty-one books and hundreds of articles, I recognize those rejections as the fruit of the gatekeepers. Not to keep riff-raff out and the elite special high-profile moneymaker folks inside. But rather, they helped maintain excellence on the "inside" of the mysterious world of publishing and offered training. Every single letter reminded me to hone my gifts, learn from my mistakes, and write the very best sentence, paragraph, article, and book possible.

Foreword

For the gatekeepers in the Old Testament with their life-or-death job, trustworthiness topped their character requirement list. Seems vital for people given the responsibility of protecting access to an important site, whether the city gates or the gates to the Temple. Many gatekeepers (okay, 212) in the Old Testament guarded the tent of meeting—the gates of the house of the Lord—from the north, south, east, and west. (See 1 Chronicles 9:22-24.)

The trustworthy experts in *Getting Past the Publishing Gatekeepers* have tended gates from all sides as well, from reader and reviewer, agent, and editor all the way to the position of publisher. Plus, they've worn their writer shoes for years. Imagine the broad spectrum of four lifetimes crammed into these readable, helpful pages. In fact, the book began among four faculty members at the Write-to-Publish conference. Hope's course on the subject drew the other three authors into the possibility: their passion and knowhow could help writers get through the gates.

This is the book we've all needed: not to figure out how to sneak through as a stealth agent, but to understand how to create books for readers, agents, editors, and publishers.

These trustworthy authors help us clear the gates' hinges; they want writers to succeed by becoming the best author with the best angles for the readers—the very ones who buy the books. Intensely practical and helpful, the following chapters show us how to invest our limited time and energy. *Gatekeepers'* authors contribute so much wisdom and experience, you are getting four books inside the cover of one. These tools will draw you past the sleep-stupor of overwhelm, whether from the vast and confusing options in social media or finding collaboration rather than competition. They answer questions you wanted to ask or didn't even know to ask. Both reasonable and realistic, each chapter concludes with primary takeaways to usher you forward.

Why buy this book? Because the world awaits the gifts you bring. These experts swing open the gates; they want to sweep you inside with their knowledge, experience, and hopes for your writing success.

Foreword

The gatekeepers' goal? Not to exclude you, but rather to create products that invite many, through your words and work, into the presence of the King.

After all, writing is a dangerous calling—truly a life-or-death position. Why? So readers' lives change. Whether good writing or bad writing, words change the world. Thanks to these gatekeepers, ours can change the world for the better.

What are you waiting for? Come on in. The gate's open.

Introduction

Aspiring-author Annie types "The End" on her manuscript, leans back in her desk chair, and sighs. She did it. She wrote a book. That's quite an accomplishment—an endeavor few people see through to the end. But as Annie will soon learn, the road leading toward the Land of Published Authors is fraught with obstacles.

Determined to join the elite ranks, Annie tucks her completed manuscript in her basket, steps onto the road, and puts one ruby-slippered foot in front of the other. Tentatively at first, but as her confidence builds, she picks up her pace, focused on her goal of finding the Great and Powerful Publisher.

Soon, she reaches a crossroads and has no idea which way to go. Luckily, a mentor steps in and guides her. But Annie quickly discovers she'll need more than a mentor to navigate past the pesky poppy fields of the publishing world. After attending an array of writers' conferences and enlisting the aid of a freelance editor (or two), she slings her arms through those of her critique partners and skips through the spooky forest.

As the woods deepen and the wicked witch of doubt casts a dark gloom over her, Annie slows her pace, coming to grips with the

Introduction

challenges standing between her and success: Agents, and Editors, and Readers, oh, my!

Finally, her goal is within sight. She steps up to the gates of the Land of Published Authors and rings the bell. When the gatekeeper pops his mustached face through the window and says, in a rather intimidating voice, "State your business," she gulps before answering.

"I've come to see the Publisher."

The gatekeeper looks aghast. "Nobody can see the Publisher!"

But Annie is determined. Besides, she's traveled so far and worked so hard. She sucks in a deep breath and stands her ground. "I'm ready to be published!"

"Prove it!" demands the gatekeeper.

Annie digs in her basket, pulls out her completed manuscript, and thrusts it toward the gatekeeper. "I did it," she says. "I wrote a whole book!"

The gatekeeper knows that tenacity is vital for admission to the Land of Published Authors, and he recognizes this trait in Annie. "Well, why didn't you say so in the first place? That's a horse of a different color!"

As Annie tiptoes through the gates, she realizes the Land of Published Authors isn't what she thought it would be. She encounters more gatekeepers—agents and editors—who insist on further preparation before she can see the Great and Powerful Publisher. After primping and polishing her manuscript to the point she barely recognizes her original story, she's finally allowed to see the Publisher face to face.

The Publisher takes a quick glance at her proposal and bellows a laugh that echoes throughout the massive chamber. "You want me to publish *THIS?* We don't need any more books in that genre. You should have submitted it last week!" Then, he demands even more of her than she thought possible. "Go kill the wicked witch of doubt and bring back an enormous author platform!"

All that work. All that effort. All the fears, challenges, time, money. Wasted. If only she'd known what publishing professionals truly wanted. If only she'd known how to get past the gatekeepers. If only she'd known she was supposed to knock and not ring the doorbell. If only ...

Nearly all aspiring authors can feel Annie's frustration. If you've journeyed along and followed the path, yet still find yourself struggling to get past the publishing gatekeepers, this book is for you.

In the following pages, you'll get a behind-the-scenes peek into the Land of Published Authors. In fact, it's not just a peek—this book will give you a guided tour. You'll learn what agents want, how to woo readers, how to entice acquisitions editors. You'll even discover how to win the heart of the Great and Powerful Publisher, which, just like the Wizard of Oz—spoiler alert—is a regular person.

This book takes the combined experience of four industry professionals—an agent, a publisher, an editor, and an influencer—and walks you through how to win the heart of each gatekeeper within the Land of Published Authors. And although it may seem like each publishing professional wants something different from authors, the truth is, we all want the same things: a great book and an author with whom we can have a great relationship.

While we can't guarantee you'll get a publishing contract by following the advice in this book, we hope the information we've shared will bring you closer to your goal.

Part One

Winning the Hearts of Agents

By Hope Bolinger

Chapter 1

Introduction to Winning the Hearts of Agents

This book first started as a class I presented at a writing conference.

I'd noticed how publishing tends to have four different gatekeepers—agents, publishers, editors, and readers/reviewers. And all of them appear to want different things. Or do they?

The class walked conferees through how to win the hearts of these gatekeepers and create a book that checked all the boxes, increasing the aspiring author's chances of getting published.

But before the conference, this book began with experience.

I've done all four roles in the industry.

- **Agent**—I worked at two different agencies over the span of four years, helping seventy books find their forever homes at publishing houses.

- **Publisher**—I worked on the pub board of several publishers. Now, I am the acquisitions editor of End Game Press.

Introduction to Winning the Hearts of Agents

- **Editor**—I freelance edited the works of two hundred-plus authors, including bestsellers, such as Jerry B. Jenkins and Michelle Medlock Adams. Working as a developmental editor, copy editor, and proofreader, I've spanned the gamut in terms of experience.

- **Reader/Reviewer**—For four years, I served as a reviewer for a library association. As an avid reader, I continue to read and review books.

When Linda Fulkerson, who wrote the publisher section of this book, suggested I turn my presentation into a book, I thought, "Why not?"

When I first dove into the industry as a writer, I had no idea which publishing professional wanted what. It seemed like agents wanted authors with platform. And publishers? Well, they asked for books that hit market trends. Editors desired polished manuscripts, and readers begged for something entirely different.

So, why not ask the industry professionals to lay it out for writers in one book?

Why not hear from an agent, a publisher, an editor, and a reviewer about how to woo them and their industry colleagues?

Linda and I reached out to Rowena Kuo, an editor, and Carrie Schmidt, a reader/reviewer, and this book was born.

We sincerely hope this guide helps you in your publishing journey. Although every industry professional operates differently, and at first glance, it appears as though each one wants something different, we are actually all searching for the same thing.

We're rooting for you, and we hope this book gives you the next steps you need to win over the hearts of the publishing industry gatekeepers, time and time again.

Chapter 2

Let's Talk about What Agents Do

The agent is perhaps the most misunderstood role among publishing industry professionals. And yet, acquiring an agent is one of the most urgent desires of many aspiring authors.

Agents didn't always exist, but they've been around for a long time. In fact, literary agencies can be traced back to the late 1800s. As technology has improved, enabling more and more writers to produce manuscripts faster and easier, the publishing world has become inundated with would-be books. And one of an agent's tasks is to weed through those works and see which are publishable. Although many small publishing houses don't require submissions to be screened and submitted by a literary agent, the larger ones do.

Some writers have complained that agents are merely an extra gatekeeper in the publishing process. But agents are much more than a speed bump between your manuscript and a publishing contract. Most authors are aware of the gatekeeper role an agent plays. And if that's all agents do, why do new authors want one so desperately? What else do they do? And how can an author win over the heart of an agent?

To answer these questions, we must first establish the definition of a "literary agent." In my four years as an agent, I found that people were often confused about an agent's role in an author's career.

A Brief-ish Definition

Literary Agent
/ˈlidəˌrerē ˈājənt/
Noun

1. A person who acts as a representative for an author or book. They will help shape a proposal and send it to publishers who are good fits for that project—primarily to publishers who only accept agented submissions.
2. A person who negotiates contracts and helps an author understand what rights the publisher is offering. Because the agent represents the author, this negotiating process can ensure the author is protected not only for this book but for future projects. Yes, the agent will consider the author's best interests, but a good agent wants *both* the author and the publisher to be happy with the deal.
3. A person who walks the book through light edits, ensuring it is ready for publication.
4. A person who makes connections with publishers, creating more prospects for an author.
5. A person who encourages an author.
6. A person who serves as a mediator between the publisher and author, after the author has signed a contract for their book.

And on and on.
Agents do a lot.
From talking authors off ledges when they receive rejections to assisting with cover design questions and issues, agents are

cheerleaders, toe-in-the-door steppers, life preservers, friends, editors, negotiators, and everything in between.

No, they do not deserve the complaints they have received from those who don't understand their role in the industry.

Yes, they wish they could take on far more than they do in terms of clientele.

And yes, they want to see you succeed. Even if they cannot guarantee your success.

Myths about Agents

Now that we've established *what* a literary agent is and some of the tasks he or she does, let's talk about some misconceptions.

- **Myth #1:** An agent will get me a book deal.

An agent can, and *should*, do whatever they can to find a home for your book.

However, they may not be able to place every single project, or even one single project, with a publishing house.

As an author, I learned this harsh reality. The moment I signed with my agent, I thought, "Great! Now those years of querying are over. Within a couple of months, I'm going to have a book deal."

Within a couple of months, I most certainly did *not* have a book deal.

It took us a solid year to place a book—and not the original book we started querying. That one never found a home.

The industry moves at a glacial pace, but having an agent can speed up the process, as publishers respond faster to agented submissions than unsolicited ones. This doesn't mean the answer will be quick, but *quicker*.

- **Myth #2:** My agent works at this full-time and makes a living from it.

Let's Talk about What Agents Do

The truth: Some agents don't work full-time as agents, and some most certainly do not make enough to live off their work.

Many agents have a full-time job elsewhere. Some agents work as editors, book coaches, or in non-industry-related jobs. Several others have retired from their day jobs and decided to "give back" to the book industry by dedicating their time to helping other authors succeed.

Even some agents who work a forty-hour week as agents scrape together a meager living. Why?

Let's do a little math, and remember, agents don't make money until you do.

- Agents work on commission. The industry standard is 15 percent of sales, including advances.
- Most small publishers have scaled back advances or don't give them at all, though a good agent almost exclusively works with publishing houses that do offer advances. Still, depending upon the contract, that advance may be doled out in stages—a portion upon signing, another installment upon receipt of the manuscript, and the remainder upon publication. All that to say, the agent may not earn a full commission on your advance right away.
- Agents may spend a lot of time helping an author prepare a manuscript before submitting it, and they don't get paid until a book deal is reached.

This means that some agents make very little at their job. And even if they do make a living from agenting, it may take years to build up their income to that level.

Agenting is a labor of love. Yes, they make money, but not as much as you would think.

- **Myth #3:** My agent will do marketing and extensive editing for me.

The truth: Most agents don't do marketing for you, and although they will offer suggestions for edits, don't expect a thorough edit worth thousands of dollars.

Yes, exceptions do exist.

Plenty of agents may offer marketing help or extensive edits, but keep in mind that most agents have the job of getting your manuscript into the hands of a publisher, negotiating the best deal, and standing by as mediator. Anything else is voluntary on the part of the agent. As agents typically have many clients, the sheer fact of *time* prevents them from getting involved heavily in editing or marketing. They also operate in their specific gifts. It's a rare agent who is exceptionally gifted in marketing or editing. And if they invest in one client's marketing strategies, how can they not be expected to do so with all their clients, or slight their efforts in other areas?

During my time as an agent, several authors asked me for marketing help.

Much as I wanted to come to their aid, at the end of it all, they discovered that marketing fell on them as an author. Or a personal assistant (PA), marketing specialist, or publicist, hired by the author. I worked several part-time jobs just to be able to stay with agenting as long as I did, and I simply didn't have the hours in my day to aid authors in "extracurriculars."

Wrapping it Up

Agents love writers. They want to see them succeed. But they can't take on every writer.

- **Takeaway One:** Agents present books to publishers who are closed to submissions from unagented writers.

They negotiate contracts, help with some light editing, encourage authors, and wear various other hats.

- **Takeaway Two:** Agents aren't the bad guys. They exist to help establish and advance an author's career. It's a labor of love that doesn't always give agents a hefty return on their investment. So, while you may need to temper your expectations somewhat, you also need to remember that your agent wants you to succeed.

Now that we've established who agents are, let's talk about how to secure representation from an agent.

Chapter 3

Let's Talk about Querying Agents

You're in line for the newest ride at the amusement park. Sunlight scorches your shoulders as you try to divert your thoughts from the pain in your calves, a result of standing too long in one place. Scents of funnel cakes and fries drift past. Your stomach gurgles as you glance back at the line snaking behind you.

No, you can't leave. Doing so will forfeit your place.

As you distract yourself by playing some variation of "Never Have I Ever" with those in line with you, you notice something out of the corner of your eye.

A woman ducks underneath the metal bars and sneaks into a gap in front of you.

Is she ... cutting in line?

Clearly, she hasn't been waiting for over an hour, like everyone else. Instead, she decided to shortcut everything and find a place closer to the ride.

Your blood sizzles. How could she?

Relief washes over you when a shout prickles your ear. A park worker yells at her to evacuate the line and leave the premises. Rules dictate that if someone cuts in line, they're barred from the amusement park for the day.

Why People Like Shortcuts

When it comes to approaching agents, many authors seem to have the same idea as the woman in our story above—"This line is taking too long. I'm going to try and cut it."

So they "try" anything from Direct Messaging agents on social media to shot-gunning submissions (more on this in a moment).

Time after time, those who "cut" in line get banned from the park, and a similar scenario occurs in the querying world. Querying takes a long-haul type of patience, and unfortunately, no one is an exception. You must stand in line with everyone else; otherwise, you risk losing your chance to win the heart of any agent.

The Fast-Passers

Just as happens in an amusement park, sometimes a fortunate few do get a legitimate pass to cut to the front of the line. Only a handful of people get this fast pass to bypass the slush pile, though. And I do mean a handful. Here are the exceptions to those who can "cut in line" the right way, without earning themselves an instant rejection.

1. **The High-Platformers**—If you have hundreds of thousands to millions of followers, you may find agents or publishers will reach out to you personally. But most of us reading this book do not fit into this category.
2. **The Conference-Goers**—Best way to connect with an agent and jump over the slush pile? Meet one at a writers' conference. There, you will get a ten-or-fifteen-minute chance to pitch your idea to an agent. If they like your pitch, they'll ask for you to send them a query or

proposal. Conference queries get prioritized in the submissions inbox.
3. **The Pitch-Partiers**—On Twitter, and a few other social media platforms, agents will occasionally make an appearance at pitch parties. During these events, if a writer tweets an elevator pitch and an agent likes that tweet, it means, "Go ahead and send it to me." At the risk of dating myself, as these fluctuate from year to year, Google the search term "Twitter pitch parties" and see the results for upcoming events. Make sure to follow the rules, though. Every "event" operates differently.

Tips for the Rest of Us

Those who don't fall into the above categories must wait in the longer line. Right?

Believe it or not, if you follow the tips below, you'll have a better chance of "getting on the ride" than 90 percent of people in the line.

Why?

As an agent, I received ten thousand submissions a year. Yes, you read that number right.

This meant that if someone did something even as simple as following my submissions guidelines, they immediately advanced ahead of nine thousand of those queries.

Let's dive into those tips right now.

- **Follow the Rules**

It sounds simple. Only send queries to agents who are accepting new clients. Send them the requested three chapters (for fiction, that's the first three chapters, for nonfiction, you can usually submit the first chapter and any other two chapters). Read the agent's guidelines about how they specifically request that you submit your query.

Let's Talk about Querying Agents

However, many authors don't take the time to read the rules for individual agencies. So, if you follow the guidelines to a *T*, you've already beaten out nine of ten submitters.

- **Really Research the Agents**

If an agent doesn't take on Dystopian right now, your Dystopian book will not convince them to change their mind. Research their clients and their clients' books. Research the agents themselves. Read their website. Their guidelines will make it clear what genres they do and do not want to see right now. Then, respect those guidelines and query only agents who *are* interested in your genre.

- **Make Sure Your Materials Are Industry-Ready**

Plenty of books in the industry and articles online will tell you how to properly write a query, proposal, one sheet, etc. So, I won't take much time covering those specific types of submissions material. But *do* make sure you have up-to-date versions of the following submissions materials:

- **One Sheet**—Often used at conferences, this is a one-page overview that details your book's premise and shares a little bit about yourself. You can adjust the formatting to fit more on this page if needed. Make your one-sheet as attractive and professional as possible. If you're not sure how to design it, you can hire someone to do that for you.
- **Query**—Think of this as a cover letter for your book. No longer than a page, this letter tells the agent what the book is about, why it's a good fit for the agent, and why you are the best person to write it.
- **Proposal**—A 15-45+ page document that explains why your book is marketable, it often includes an author bio,

platform information, comparable titles (books published within the last five years, similar to yours), your marketing plan, a synopsis (for fiction) or chapter outline (for nonfiction), and three chapters.
- **Partial**—When an agent requests to see part of your manuscript, they will specify exactly what they want. It can be anything from the first three chapters to the first fifty pages.
- **Full**—In certain cases, an agent will request to see your entire manuscript. So, unless you write adult nonfiction, which can sometimes be contracted on the proposal alone, make sure your manuscript is finished *and* polished before you audition for agents.

Submissions No-Nos

Want to reach the front of the line? Make sure to avoid the following:

- **Shot-Gunning Submissions**

Understandably, writers can sometimes lose patience on this long, and often tedious, journey to publication. Some will include two hundred agents in the same email, and the email will go something like this: "Here's my book. Who wants it?"

Querying is a lot like applying for a job. As such, you must personalize your cover letter for each employer you're applying to. If you send your résumé to two hundred employers in the same email, you may have just eradicated yourself from that industry. The same can be true for trying to avoid the line by querying two hundred agents at once.

- **Retaliating**

No one likes to get rejected. No one. We've all been there.

At the time of writing this chapter, I have 1400 bylines, twenty books under contract, and have contributed to ten other books. I also have received thousands of rejections, and each one still stings.

But if an agent rejects you, kindly send them a "thank you" email for their time and move on.

If you reply with a passive-aggressive message about how they clearly didn't read enough to make an informed decision, they will remember you. And not in a good way.

- **Bargaining**

No means no.

Don't try to convince the agent to read more. Don't ask what changes you can make to convince them to turn their no into a yes.

Keep in mind, most agents go through thousands of submissions a year. If they said, "No, thanks," respect their wishes.

In this same vein, don't ask for a referral either. It makes no sense to ask an employer to pass you along to a competitor if they rejected you for a job. The same rules apply to publishing.

- **Checking in Too Soon**

Agents tend to give standard check-in times—anywhere from six-to-eight weeks to ninety days or more.

If you badger them every week about submissions updates, they may decide they don't want to work with you. No one wants a high-maintenance client.

Submissions Yes-Yes-es

Although it won't fast-pass you in the line, these tips will help you be remembered as kind and easy to work with in a very small industry. An industry that talks.

- **Thanking Them**

Like all of us, agents remember kind people. Especially if it was a close call and the agent ended up saying no. When I was an agent, if someone wrote me a nice note, I remembered them.

And if an agent or publisher asks about that author, odds are good that they will give him or her high praise. I know I certainly did with a number of authors.

- **Knowing When You're Close And When You're Not**

If you've received many full requests and personalized feedback (meaning, they took the time to write you a note about some areas to fix in your manuscript), you're close. If you've only received form rejections and no requests for the full, your manuscript likely needs more work. Revise and polish it and get feedback from your critique partners or hire a freelance editor before re-submitting.

- **Budgeting Your Submissions**

What I mean by this is that you shouldn't send out all of your submissions at once. Because if you get rejected by every agent on your list, then what?

Try ten agents and see what happens. If they don't bite, rework your book and then query ten more.

- **Constantly Investing in Your Craft and Platform**

Agents can tell who reads within their genre, and who reads *recently published works* in their genre.

They can tell who spends hours working on their writing craft.

Who is trying their best to grow their platform, no matter how small.

Who can take direction.

Agents can see those things almost right away.

If an applicant wants to earn the job, he or she must become as ready as possible for that particular line of work.

So, stick with it for the long haul, the long line. The ride will be worth the wait. I promise.

Wrapping it Up

The submissions process really isn't that complicated. I think—speaking from a writer's perspective—that we simply just don't like to hear about how much time and work it takes.

The traditional publishing industry asks us to give it our all—and more. And many of us want to believe we're the exception.

We're not.

- **Takeaway One:** Don't shortcut anything. That will earn you an instant rejection, and no one likes a line-cutter. Especially agents. Respect their guidelines out of respect for them and their expertise.

- **Takeaway Two:** Kindness and patience go a long way. In this small industry, everyone talks. Make sure they speak well of you.

- **Takeaway Three:** Invest in craft, platform, and research. Agents want to work with those who do the homework. No, you don't need millions of followers. But you do need to prove how you can stand out from the tens of thousands of submissions a single agency receives each year.

Let's say you do manage to stand out and get a bite. More than a bite—suppose an agent requests your full manuscript and wants to get on a call with you. In our next chapter, we'll discuss how to handle the next step of the process.

Chapter 4

Let's Talk about "The Call"

You have an interview today. But not for yourself. Well, not exactly.

You check your outfit one again and notice a wrinkle. Hopefully that won't show up on the video call, scheduled for one minute from now. You click on the link, breath hitching, and check your appearance once more in the web camera.

Here goes nothing.

Whirring sounds from your laptop as the picture loads of the literary agent on the other side of the screen. She shoves her glasses up her nose and smiles at you.

"Let's talk about your book."

What Is "The Call"

The Call happens after an agent has requested your full manuscript.

Or in the case of nonfiction, they've reviewed your proposal materials and deemed your submission ready enough for The Call.

Let's Talk about "The Call"

Perhaps the agent sent some additional questions for you to answer, perhaps not.

In either case, you've gone through many rounds of communication with them by this point, and now you've arrived at The Call stage.

During this interview, an agent will determine if you are a good fit for one another. They may tease out some plot points in your book, ask you about other books you've worked on, or want to know more about your personality.

But here's the thing most authors don't know about The Call.

Authors have the opportunity to use The Call to interview the agent. You heard me right.

If any of us have participated in a job interview—and I will operate under the assumption that most of us have—we know that the interview is a litmus test for what our future working environment will look like. Does our interviewer seem enthusiastic about the workplace? Do they balk when we ask about overtime and expectations for the workers?

The same goes for The Call.

We want to determine if we "click" with the agent.

So, in this chapter, let's go over what agents look for on the call, what questions to ask, and what to do after The Call.

What Agents Look For

Every agent differs on what they want to see, but most can agree they will look for the following on The Call.

- **That You're Not Crazy**

Sorry, but if you step into an agent's submissions inbox and see some of the weird things some authors do to their characters in the fictional books they query ... you can understand why agents may exercise caution.

Some authors can, for lack of a better word, get a little finicky or even arrogant when it comes to their work. Although agents do understand how much an author has invested in their book, they want to make sure they spot professionalism in The Call.

- **That You Have Realistic Expectations**

The agent will likely ask what you expect them to do with your books.

Bad Answer: Make me super famous, get me movie deals, and Big Five contracts, while I kick back and relax. Oh, and I expect you to do all the editing and marketing for me too. For free.

Good Answer: Shop the books—that you deem ready for sale—to publishers in your sphere of influence who you think would be a good fit. In the meantime, I will do everything I can to pre-market my books and have them as polished as I can make them.

Agents can only do so much. They will try their very best to find a home for your book—after all, they truly want authors to succeed. They care about great books and desire to place manuscripts in the hands of the best publisher for each work. But they must compete in a crowded industry and want to see patience and hard work on your end.

- **That You're a Personality Who Is Pleasant to Work With**

I know, this sounds harsh. Especially if you've put plenty of time into your marketing, platform, editing, and craft. But an agent-author relationship works a lot like a marriage. You do want just the right fit.

Don't worry, you can measure the agent's temperament in The Call too.

Agents will also gauge if you take feedback well. They may mention edits they foresee in your manuscript. Or they may discuss areas of your platform or marketing that need work.

Show your flexibility. That you will do whatever is asked of you. Agents operate with a business mindset, and they want to make your "product" as appealing as possible to publishers.

Questions You Should Ask on the Call

Keep in mind that you want to interview the agent too.

An agent can help you develop your career as well as place your book (and future books) with publishers. Approach this meeting as an opportunity for developing a career-long relationship. You want to make sure you put your work and career in the right hands. Below, I've included some questions to ask and why you should ask these.

- **Question One:** Are you just representing this book, or others?

Some agents only represent one work. Most intend to work with an author for a lifetime (or for the duration of the author-agency agreement). Determine this on The Call.

- **Question Two:** Do I have to stick with one genre?

If you want to genre-jump, be sure to ask this, but understand that an author's desire to write in multiple genres places the agent in an awkward position. Publishers invest time, money, and other resources to brand an author. It's difficult to brand a genre-jumper. And even some of the most successful authors (Think: John Grisham's *The Painted House*) suffered career setbacks when they abandoned a strong brand. So, yes, ask this question if you are serious about a multi-genre career, but understand an agent has space for only so many clients, and this may make you a less appealing prospect.

- **Question Three:** Will you send out multiple books at one time?

Submissions can take a long time. Sometimes agents do send out multiple books at a time. Sometimes they don't. While you're on The Call, be sure to ask the agent to explain scenarios that would warrant a single submission instead of multiple ones.

- **Question Four:** How do you prefer to communicate with clients?

Some agents like calls. Others prefer emails.
Although some agents will cater communications preferences to clients, many won't, and there are reasons for this. Perhaps the agent works from home and his or her spouse and children are also there. Other reasons could include time zone differences. Meetings. Travel. The list goes on. Be flexible and be willing to discuss what works best for the agent you sign with.

- **Question Five:** How many clients do you have?

Some agents list their clientele on their websites; some don't, perhaps for privacy reasons. Each agent operates differently, and as mentioned before, not all agents work their business full time. The number of clients itself doesn't explain the entire story, though, as each client may be in a different place in his or her career. Other agents may work in an agency and have support staff, so they can handle more clients.

- **Question Six:** What happens if my book doesn't sell?

None of us enjoy thinking about our books not finding a home. But sadly, try as they might, agents may not successfully place every manuscript in the market. Consider, instead, asking what the initial period would be for the agent-author agreement, and, if both parties are agreeable, could that agreement be renewed when the period lapses before a book has been placed.

- **Question Seven:** If we have to part ways, what does that look like?

If a call goes well, an agent will likely send a contract. And the written agreement should spell this out. But it doesn't hurt to hear it from the agent's own words. If either the agent or author feels the need to dissolve the agreement, what would that entail?

- **Question Eight:** What questions do you have for me?

Likely, plenty. But if for some reason they haven't asked you any, throw this one into the conversation.

The Internet is full of blogs that detail several more questions to ask agents. The Call can last anywhere from fifteen minutes to over an hour. Prepare for this as you would prepare for a job interview.

And if The Call goes well, be prepared for the next steps.

What You Should Do After The Call

First, wait. You need an agreement in hand before you can do anything else. And if an agent sends a contract, ask how long you have to make a decision.

Most will give you about two weeks.

When this happens, you will review the agreement (more on this in the next chapter).

Then, you may simultaneously reach out to some of the agent's clients to ask them about their experiences. Assure them that they will remain anonymous. That way they can speak freely.

Before an author sends out queries, it's important to have thoroughly researched the agencies you plan to submit to, so when an agent does offer to represent you, you will be ready. You are under no obligation to accept an offer of representation, so if you aren't comfortable, then don't. But if you choose to accept an agent's offer, be professional and reach out to the remaining agents you've queried to let them know you have been offered an agreement with another agency.

Wrapping it Up

Before you receive The Call, really, before you even submit a query, do your research, and don't submit to any agent you wouldn't be willing to be represented by. Don't waste your time and theirs by querying someone who wouldn't be a good fit for your work. Then, when The Call comes, you can enjoy the thrill that the hard work of polishing your manuscript and researching agents and crafting a compelling query letter has been worth it.

- **Takeaway One:** The agent will determine your level of professionalism and flexibility on The Call. They want to make sure that you have realistic expectations for them and that you will be a good fit for each other.

- **Takeaway Two:** On The Call, it's fine to ask the agent to clarify things you don't understand and to ask questions so you can get to know them better. However, remember that The Call is a conversation—not an interrogation.

- **Takeaway Three:** Authors, especially those who are new with little track record or platform, are in no position to make demands of a potential agent. There are far more authors seeking representation than there are agents with available slots.

Chapter 5

Let's Talk about the Agency Contract

Getting a contract is like receiving a box of chocolates. Sometimes you grab the most delicious dark chocolate filled with raspberry creme—and if you hate that flavor ... just pretend you like it for now.

But unfortunately, sometimes you get the one stuffed with apricot jam.

And if you enjoy that one, I'm sorry to say that we can't be friends.

Although the vast majority of agents are wonderful and desire to help authors grow their careers, there are, as in any industry, some bad ones.

In this chapter, we'll go over what to look for in an agency contract, and how to avoid those apricot chocolates.

Should I Hire an Attorney?

I get this question from authors a lot.

To answer this question, "No, but it never hurts." In fact, as an

Let's Talk about the Agency Contract

agent, I told many of my clients to have an attorney review the agency contract before they signed with me.

A good author-agent agreement is designed to be mutually beneficial to both the author and the agent/agency. If you, as an author, are unsure of the contract's details or language, having a professional look over the terms is a good idea.

For those who cannot afford legal advice, or just want to go through the agreement without assistance ... what should you look for in the contract?

Agreement Duration

Every author-agent agreement includes a section that lays out the term of the contract.

Some terms may be for a year. Others, two-plus years. No matter how long the term, the agreement should also include a termination clause.

Why?

As an agent, I never wanted my clients to be unhappy. If they felt the relationship didn't work between us, I allowed them to cancel our agreement before our contract expired. All the good agents feel the same way. They're there to help.

None took me up on that offer, but it was there.

Sadly, an unethical agent may say that you cannot cancel the contract as an author. That only *they* have the ability to end the relationship prior to the end of the agreement. This could lead to some sticky situations down the road. Because if you change your mind, you can't wriggle out until you reach the end of the term. Make sure you understand your rights, and if there isn't a clause that allows for an author to cancel the agreement, request that it be revised to include that. If the agent refuses, then this isn't a good agent in the first place. Don't sign the agreement. Look for a legitimate, ethical agent.

Other agents may also say that, yes, you can make a clean break.

But the clause adds that a client cannot send or place his/her book with another agency for a specific period of time—typically sixty days, but sometimes it can be longer, perhaps six months.

Why is that included, and what should an author do when reviewing the agreement?

The reason agencies include the gap between representation is to allow time for them to reach out to any editors who currently are reviewing your manuscripts. This is a period to tie up loose ends, not to continue pitching your book.

Have the agent spell out the termination clause clearly in the contract, making sure you can also have a say as to when you end the relationship. If they have the six-month clause, as mentioned above, see if you can negotiate it to a shorter period.

If they refuse, ask if they are willing to dissolve it if you manage to get another agent before the six months.

If they still balk without giving a reason, it may be best to sign with a different agent.

Authors need to understand that agents have the right to dissolve the agreement as well. What might prompt an agent to end the contract before the term expires? If a client doesn't submit proposals to pitch, doesn't accept critique, goes rogue on social media, creates problems for other publishing professionals, etc., it makes good business sense for the agency to cut ties.

Remember, professionalism on both parts—the author's and the agent's—make for a successful business relationship.

A Renewal

Author-agent agreements should also spell out what happens when you reach the end of the term.

Will they renew the contract? Will they make a decision on a case-by-case basis? They may not state this in the agreement, but it never hurts to ask them.

A Percentage

Fifteen percent.

Agents in North America take fifteen percent (in some rare cases, less than that) of your advance and any royalties you get from sales.

If an agent takes more than that, (unless in the rare cases of foreign or film rights, which are often handled differently), shop for another agent.

If an agent charges you any money upfront, run. Ethical agents don't charge you fees—they earn a commission on your royalties. Again, an agent doesn't make money unless you do. So, it's in their best interest to help you develop your career and negotiate the best possible publishing contract for your books. Agents invest a lot of time and resources to help authors succeed. Those who require reading fees, submission fees, or any fee other than the industry standard royalty commission, are possibly unethical and certainly not among the majority of upstanding, helpful agents.

If an agent tries to get you to pay them for supplementary services such as book coaching, editing, marketing, etc., run.

If an agent charges writers for other services, with the hopes of eventually making them their clients, run.

Whew, that's a lot of running.

As an agent, I also did freelance editing for authors. However, I knew that could quickly end in a conflict of interest if any of them wanted to become my clients. Therefore, I made it clear on my editing website that, "If I edit your book, I cannot take you on as a literary agent client. That would be a clear conflict of interest. Agents should not make any money off of authors until they land them a contract. Then they take fifteen percent of any royalties."

Agents don't make much money. But that doesn't mean they should take advantage of authors. And thankfully, most don't.

Best Efforts?

Often, an agent will include a clause that essentially says, "We will do our best to find your book a home. This doesn't guarantee we'll be successful. But we'll try our hardest."

You could ask them to spell out in writing what this means. Will they shop the manuscript every few months? Will they get on regular meetings with publishers to find out *exactly* what they want? Will they make sure you polish your work before they present it to the industry gatekeepers? (Tip: Your proposal should be as polished as possible *before* submitting it to an agent. Otherwise, you likely won't find a good one willing to represent you.)

Even if their intended actions are listed in the agreement, you can still ask them about it if you don't yet feel that you have at least a general sense of what "best efforts" means to this particular agent.

Make sure you get an agent who fights for you. After all, you fought hard to get in front of them in the first place. And the "fight" goes both ways. It's hard for an agent to fight for an author who has an entitled attitude or one who won't do his or her part of the work (completing suggested revisions, meeting deadlines, etc.).

Wrapping it Up

When an agent signs an agreement with an author, understand that your new agent is about to pour many hours into your work, with the hopes of finding the best possible publishing home for your books.

- **Takeaway One:** Although it's not necessary to have an attorney go over your contract, it never hurts. An agency agreement requires, at minimum, a few months of holding your book exclusively under that agency. So, before you sign, understand both your rights and those of the agent.

Let's Talk about the Agency Contract

- **Takeaway Two:** How an agent handles negotiations now will tell you how they work with publishers. As a publisher now (after doing agenting for four years), I can tell you that there are certain agents I will not work with, because they make the contract process so difficult.

- **Takeaway Three:** Make sure everything is in writing. Contract clauses can be vague. Have your future-hopeful-agent spell everything out in the agreement. Request that all terms are clarified. Better to ask and understand everything clearly than to feel as though you are entering an agreement flying blind.

However, let's say you got one of those wonderful raspberry chocolates. You sign the contract and kick back and relax, right? Wrong.

The agent expects you to do some things in the meantime. And in the same vein, you should have some expectations for them too. Our next chapter will discuss those in detail.

Chapter 6

Let's Talk about Expectations (On Both Sides)

You've decided to play a game of tennis with a doubles partner. Never mind that you've never stepped onto a court before, you want to give the game a try. And you've seen it on TV plenty of times. How hard can it be?

Although the scoring makes no sense, you and your partner appear to be failing. You realize, several minutes into a set, why. Instead of getting all the volleys at the net, your partner has chosen to swat her racquet at a swarm of bees.

"What's the matter with you?" You ask through gritted teeth when another ball claps against her feet. One more point for the other team. "You have to get all the net shots. That's how doubles works."

At least, you think so, based on what you've seen.

She tightens her grip on her racquet and shoots you a frustrated glance. "You didn't even bring a racquet." She gestures at your arms. "How are you supposed to play tennis with that *thing*?"

You glance down at the baseball bat you've brought to the match. *That* would explain the lack of groundstrokes you've been able to get to during the games.

Let's Talk about Expectations (On Both Sides)

No wonder you and your partner are losing. You're not working together for success.

Great Expectations

An agenting-author relationship works a lot like a tennis doubles match.

You must compete against two very good players—publishers and readers. And sometimes it seems as though the odds are stacked against you.

For those of you who never had the misfortune of spending three hours a day playing tennis outside in the heat of summer—trying to make the high school Varsity team (definitely not speaking from personal experience)—doubles in tennis relies on collaboration.

Even if you have all the skills in the world, a bad partner can sink a match faster than water in a garbage disposal.

How do we, then, create the perfect partnership, so we have any fighting chance of winning the "match"?

Expectations exist for both the author and the agent. We'll discuss what *you* can expect your agent to do, and what *they* expect from you. Neither of you can win the match without the dedicated effort of both players.

What You Can Expect from Your Agent

Agents juggle a lot of balls in the air, and they need a variety of skills. They must excel at volleying, groundstrokes, serving, overhead lobs—you name it.

Although no agent will reach perfection (just as no author will, either), you can guarantee a good doubles partner will aid you in the following ways.

- **Doing Market Research**

The market changes every year, sometimes on a monthly basis.

If an agent doesn't have a pulse on the industry, they may send the book to the wrong publisher. Or they might request that you edit a book in an outdated way.

A good agent can tell you, "We can't shop this project because the market no longer takes on this type of genre. However, we can shop *this* book because I've seen more industry professionals asking for similar works."

Bad agents will send out everything in the hopes that something sticks.

Now, that doesn't mean you have a bad agent if he or she queries most of what you send them. But you should be able to tell that they are exercising discernment and operating out of what they've researched.

A great question to ask them on The Call is, "How do you stay up to date on what's happening within the publishing industry?"

- **Expanding Their Networks**

In the same vein, the industry has a very high turnover rate. Someone may work as an editor at a house one day—reviewing your full manuscript—and the next day, they send a note that tells you they are leaving that publisher or shifting roles.

If an agent only ever sends a manuscript to the *same* ten people, they are doing their clients a disservice. The emails may not even reach the right person, because certain inboxes have gone defunct.

Good agents seek to expand their network regularly. They reach out to newer editors at houses they trust, newer houses that look promising, and they even check in with trusted editors to see what they're looking for.

Spoiler alert: The needs of publishing houses change constantly. An editor may ask for sweet romance one month—get inundated with

Let's Talk about Expectations (On Both Sides)

sweet romance submissions—and then no longer want that type of work. Your agent needs to know this.

- **Pitching You Judiciously**

We'll cover this more in the "Submissions Strategies" chapter, but an agent should be sending out your work. However, they need to query the appropriate people within their network.

Similar to your initial querying process with agents, an agent should email a handful of editors ... and wait for the feedback. Based on those responses, they can decide if the book needs revisions or if they ought to shop it around more.

During all this time, your agent will report back what the publishers say—more on this in the next chapter on Communications.

- **Light Editing***

*Sometimes this looks like skimming your manuscript and giving you some pointers.

Few agents will give you an in-depth edit. But most agents give some kind of industry-standard feedback on your book before sending it out to publishers. Why? Because agents know which books are ready to place and which ones need more work.

They can help cater your book to be more palatable to publishers and give you the best chance at placing it.

- **Contract Negotiations**

In most cases, an agent is not a lawyer. However, they know what to look for in a publishing agreement.

Agents will watch for several things, including vague clauses, your advance, how many copies you get, termination clauses, and more. An agent's goal is to get you the best deal possible—while maintaining a good working relationship and an excellent reputation among industry professionals.

Agents will differ on how aggressive they act during this stage of the process, but publishers don't have time to work with someone who argues with them over every jot and tittle.

- **Mediation**

Once your book finds a home, the agent's job isn't finished. She needs to be on standby. If you are unhappy with the cover, the edits, or anything else that has a major impact on your book, you can request that your agent step in.

Agents ensure you stay protected throughout the process. And a publisher is more likely to listen to the gentle complaint of an agent, over an irate email from a dissatisfied author.

What Your Agent Expects from You

Whew, your agent does a lot for you! This means that in a good doubles partnership, it's unfair for you to sit back and relax. You also have a lot of work to do.

An agent expects you to:

- **Stay Up-to-Date on Trends**

Just as an agent does their market research, authors need to do the same.

Read recently published works in your genre. This can help you brainstorm future projects and give you some sales leads for which publishers you'd like your agent to query.

What do you mean by this, Hope?

What I mean is, maybe you stumbled across a book that just released. And it has very similar themes to yours (although yours still fits a gap in the market that this book doesn't). You flip to the acknowledgements and see which acquisitions editor took on the book.

You message your agent and say, "Hey, this person takes on similar books. Can we try querying them?"

Some agents, toward the beginning of the querying process, may even ask you to list dream publishers for your book. Make sure to do your research ahead of time so you can give them a list of houses and *specific* editors. (Tip: Make sure you spell each editor's name correctly.)

- **Working on Your Next Book**

Your first book may not place at a house.

Y'all, I have twenty-one books under contract at the time of writing this, and my first book *Lukewarm* was never placed. (To be honest, praise the Lord. It needs major work).

If you have nothing else to give your agent, and they can't find a home for Book One, then they can't do anything more for you at this point. Remember, there are way more authors out there seeking representation from agents than there are agent slots available. Be a client your agent is glad to represent by giving them solid options to work with.

During my time at the agency, some of the other agents would complain to me about clients who had no backup work in case Plan A didn't work out. Some clients would even beg them to help brainstorm ideas.

But, as we've mentioned earlier, a good agent's goal isn't just to place one (or maybe two) books, but to help develop an author's career. Make it easier for them to do that.

- **Polishing Your Work**

An agent can only help so much in the editing process.

Remember, some of them work a full-time job apart from agenting and don't have time to give you an in-depth content edit.

Even though they will read through your full manuscript, they can't catch every misspelling and missing comma.

Sending your manuscript to a professional editor or critique group or beta reader falls on you, the author. Make sure you submit to your agent something that they can represent well. Publishers get thousands of submissions. Make it difficult for them to say no to yours.

- **Building Your Platform**

Collective groaning noises

Yes, I know. As an author, I hate it too. But as I mentioned earlier, publishers receive countless submissions. I can attest to this, as I have worked for several publishers including the one where I currently work.

The number one infraction? Bad writing, followed by lack of platform—especially if you write nonfiction.

Agents expect you to expand your marketing network while they shop your books. Make sure to build your platform every month, every week, every day—a little bit at a time.

- **Being Flexible**

An agent may not land you at a dream publisher. In fact, they may place you at a smaller house than you'd hoped for.

Agents help open doors that authors could not on their own. But if your literary agent can't place you with your dream publisher, they place you with a mid-sized house, which may actually turn into your dream publisher.

When I first got an agent, I made the mistake of thinking that she would get me into a Big Five house within months. Over a year later, we placed my second book with a smaller house. It happens.

Let's Talk about Expectations (On Both Sides)

I was new and had to prove myself.

Your agent will do their best but know that the industry is tougher and far slower than most newcomers realize. A little flexibility goes a long way.

- **Represent Them Well**

When you get a contract and work with a publishing house, you still represent the agency. If you throw tantrums, nitpick edits, and send angry emails to the editors, it tells the publisher:

"Hey, so, this agency gave us this author. We no longer want to work with this author, and we may no longer want to work with this agency either."

Sadly, it *can* work that way, no matter how kind the agent.

Make sure to make your agent proud, and never, never, never burn bridges.

Wrapping it Up

Expectations go both ways. And although you can't guarantee your agent will find your book a home, if you both put in the right amount of effort, you can definitely increase your chances.

- **Takeaway One:** Expectations work like a game of tennis doubles. A weak partner can cost both the whole game. In the same way, a lazy agent or a lazy writer can prevent a book from ever finding a home.

- **Takeaway Two:** Agents shouldn't have a stagnant network. Although they continually bolster the connections they already have, industry roles change. Good agents stay on top of trends and editor wants.

Getting Past the Publishing Gatekeepers

- **Takeaway Three:** You, as the author, also have a lot of work to do. While your agent sends out your work, be reading, be working on your next book, be building your platform, and do your research too. Make sure to represent your agency well.

As your book is out on submission, your agent will communicate with you. In our next chapter, we'll cover how often, and what it looks like.

Chapter 7

Let's Talk about Communications with Your Agent

You may go weeks without hearing from your agent, but you shouldn't go months.

Every agent will communicate a little differently, but you should get news occasionally.

This brief chapter will go over communication expectations.

Communications Preferences

As we mentioned in The Call chapter, every agent prefers a different style of communication. Some enjoy phone calls; others want email only.

Make sure to adhere to what they request, or you may wind up with an exasperated agent.

If they don't like texts, don't text them. Don't find them on social media and ask them about your submissions. Respect communication boundaries.

As an agent, I dedicated specific office hours to my clients. So, whenever a client overstepped and Direct Messaged me on

Instagram or texted me, I reminded them to email me during office hours, which I sent to them again.

Some authors may imagine that they're the only client an agent has. Therefore, in their minds, their agent has plenty of time to dedicate to them, and them alone.

In reality, an agent can have anywhere from a few to dozens of clients. Authors need to respect the communications preferences agents have established and wait for them to respond as they are able.

With this in mind, when do (and should) agents communicate with authors?

When Agents Should Communicate with You

First and foremost, you should probably hear from your agent every few months. Even if they don't have any submissions information to send you, it's good practice to touch base periodically.

Apart from check-ins, you'll also hear from agents in the following ways.

- **Agent Newsletters**

Often sent monthly, an agent will keep their client pool up to date about industry trends. Here, they may congratulate clients who have new releases or have just found a publishing home for a book.

Yes, this does count as "communication" from your agent, but it shouldn't be the only communication you hear from them within the span of months.

- **Submissions Updates**

Every time a publisher rejects you ...
Every time an agent sends you out to more houses ...
Every time you get a full request ...
Every time a publisher sends feedback on your manuscript ...

Every time a publisher offers a contract ...

Every time an agent checks in with publishers after they haven't heard back for a long time ...

You should know, and you should know as many details as possible.

No matter how your agent approaches these updates, they *should* keep you in the loop. You shouldn't wonder where you stand with certain houses.

- **Delays**

If your agent didn't send out one of your books, you should know why.

Maybe the market doesn't want a story like that at this time. Maybe the agent thinks the book needs revisions.

Whatever the case, a good agent will give you reasons as to why they haven't yet contacted publishers about your proposal.

- **Just Checking In***

*Not every agent will do this.

As an agent, I would often reach out to clients who weren't on submission. Maybe they didn't have Book Two ready yet, and Book One had already found a home. As a Christian agent, I would often ask my Christian clients how I could pray for them. (For my non-Christian clients, I would ask how I could encourage them.)

An agent may also check in to see your progress on your next book. Good agents desire to work with authors for life—with the exception of agents who work with one book at a time. Therefore, they want to know the status of the next book they'll be sending to publishers.

Let's Talk about Communications with Your Agent

When Should I Check in with Them?

If you haven't heard back from your agent in months, and you have a book out on submission, then check in with them.

However, some clients can take communications expectations too far.

An agent friend of mine had a client who expected her to email once a week with updates.

"That didn't make any sense to me," my agent friend told me. "It takes publishers a long time to respond. I wouldn't even *have* an update for her that often."

Keep in mind your agent's boundaries and their budget of time. Agents have many clients and may not always have quick updates for you. But if you don't hear back for a long time, it doesn't hurt to check in.

An agent should never seem too busy for you. I knew of an agency where the clients were scared to follow up with the agent, because they'd heard stories of other agents with clients who were deemed too "high-maintenance." Some of those rumors said an agent's clients had supposedly received the boot if they emailed to ask why nothing had been sent out.

Clients shouldn't live in fear of their agent, but the author should still handle everything with professionalism and follow the agent's guidelines.

Wrapping it Up

Agents may not talk to you every week, but they should send an email every few weeks or so. Publishing can crawl at a snail's pace, though, so this can differ from agent to agent.

- **Takeaway One:** Agents should *always* keep you in the loop about submissions. You should know who has your work, who has rejected you, why they rejected you, who requested fulls, etc. Even if they cushion the blow of a rejection, you should get the general gist of why the publisher said no.

- **Takeaway Two:** Agents will often send newsletters to keep their clients, as a whole, in the loop about agenting operations. These newsletters can also show how agents are hard at work and expanding their networks to get their clients more deals.

- **Takeaway Three:** Respect an agent's business hours and boundaries. Don't DM them or text them—unless they've given you the okay to do so. Also, have realistic expectations when it comes to communications. Most agents won't send updates every week.

As an agent sends out your work, let's talk about submissions strategies next.

Chapter 8

Let's Talk about Submissions Strategies

You can win a game of chess in more than one way. It all boils down to strategy.

In the same way, agents may approach submissions differently. At the end of the day, however, we can divide how they "play the game" into two categories.

Good Submissions Strategies
and
Bad Submissions Strategies

As our knight takes a rook, let's discuss these two more in depth.

But before that ...

How can you know if your agent is implementing a good or bad strategy?

Well, if you did the research that we discussed earlier in this section, you would only sign with a reputable, above-board agent whose desire is to help you build your career. The majority of literary agents are respected, honest, and hard-working, and you can trust them to know the best strategies for your submissions.

One thing authors *can* do, if they do have concerns is network with authors outside their agent's clientele and feel them out for the way their agent handles submissions. You may find out that your agent is exactly on track, and you weren't seeing it from their perspective. You may also find out that your concerns were well-founded, but again if you've signed with the right kind of agent this shouldn't be the case.

Good Submissions Strategies

Submissions to publishers are similar to submissions to agents. It comes down to researching, customizing queries, and a little bit of all-in-the-right timing.

Let's explore some good submissions strategies.

- **Sending Out Only a Handful**

An agent needs to see how publishers react to your manuscript. If they send out your book to, let's say, five to ten people, they can judge from there how your book will fare in the broader market.

If most publishers send feedback or ask to see the whole thing, your book is on the right track.

If most reject it, oh well. Your agent will send it back to you to edit.

- **Customizing Submissions**

The materials required for a submission can differ from publisher to publisher. Some want just a proposal. Some ask for the full up front, etc.

No matter what the case, your agent will keep spreadsheets or lists that detail these wants from publishers and how to submit to them.

Agents who want a good relationship with a publisher, have to respect communications boundaries, too.

- **Getting on Meetings**

Because the needs of a publishing house can change, it doesn't hurt to have meetings with an acquisitions team. Meeting face-to-face with someone can help build the agent's relationship with that publishing team, and these conversations also convey far more than an email can.

An agent would send the best proposal possible, and if the editor is interested, the editor may ask the agent to set up a call.

- **Handling Everything with Kindness and Professionalism**

Kindness goes a long, long way in this industry.

Publishers, too, wish they could take on every manuscript. But most only have a few slots per year to fill, if that. They have no choice but to be picky. Good agents understand this and respond to rejections in a kind, professional manner. Publishers will remember that if they have a future opening that may fit one of the agent's authors.

- **Checking In**

An agent should check in after not hearing back from a publisher if it's been longer than normal since the proposal was sent. Submissions can get lost. Publishers may have thought they responded to something when the email got left in Draft mode. Things happen.

Your agent will check in if they haven't heard back from an

editor, but it is the policy of some publishing houses that their non-response is a "no." If they want a project, they will ask for more. If they don't they won't respond.

Bad Submissions Strategies

There's an old saying, "One bad apple can spoil the barrel." The same goes for agents. One unethical agent can cause a stir among author groups throughout social media, spreading the idea that all agents are bad—authors beware! Jumping to such judgments is unfair to those who work hard to help authors succeed.

Good agents provide a needed service to authors and publishers. Good agents help overcome the unfair stigma by avoiding the following list of poor submissions strategies.

Because those bad apples do exist, it's necessary to cover some bad submissions strategies and how they can serve as a detriment to agents and their clients.

- **Sending Everything Out at Once**

For any given book, an agent likely has somewhere between twenty to one hundred houses where they can try to place the project (more likely at the lower end).

If they submit your book to every place at once, they can ruin the chance of you getting a contract. Maybe the book isn't ready yet. Maybe you forgot to write chapter sixty-three, and every publisher noticed this. Maybe, maybe, maybe ...

In chess, you don't break out all the good moves at the beginning. Good strategy takes patience and particularity.

- **Not Checking Guidelines**

At one point, your agent likely checked the submissions guidelines of a publisher.

But these wish lists may change. Maybe they wanted Contemporary YA last week, and this week, they want Romantic Suspense.

Good agents do a spot-check of guidelines before they submit to publishers. If not, they may end up giving your book to a place that no longer even wants that type of book.

- **Not Reading the Books They Query**

This sounds straightforward. But it's one of those bad apple policies.

If a book is full of misspellings, at best—or objectionable content, at worst—this can reflect poorly on the agency. Publishers may get a bad taste in their mouths and may not want to work with that agent again.

- **Having a Bad Attitude**

Publishing is all about relationships.

Even if an agent does not want to work with a publisher again, the situation must be handled with tact and grace. Because industry professionals talk, your reputation really can precede you.

- **Checking in Excessively**

Checking in too often with a publisher can create frustration and reduce the chances of a book being accepted.

Different publishers operate differently. Most publishers have pub board meetings, and in many cases, an editorial board meeting is the first step. Then, if a proposal passes that step, it will go to the pub board. In most cases, each member of the pub board reads through the proposal and sample chapters. As you can see, the process can take a long time.

Good agents build relationships (how many times has that word

Let's Talk about Submissions Strategies

been mentioned?) with publishers and know the appropriate check-in frequency for each house.

Wrapping it Up

Agenting is all about strategy. Agents always want to end up in the good graces of publishers and hope to work with them time and time again. It all boils down to how much professionalism they use in the submissions process, including the preparedness of the author's manuscript to the agent's submissions practices.

- **Takeaway One:** An author should ask about an agent's submission strategy *before* signing with them.

- **Takeaway Two:** Some good strategies include following the guidelines, setting up meetings, and operating with kindness. Relationships trump the sting of rejections in this industry. Far better for an agent to preserve a good rapport with a publisher than to react unprofessionally when their client's manuscript doesn't get accepted.

- **Takeaway Three:** Bad strategies include not reading guidelines or staying up to date, burning bridges, and sending out submissions to every publishing house at once. Like a game of chess, an agent wins by playing the long game.

So, let's say you have an agent who doesn't click with you. How do you break it off?

In our final chapter, we'll discuss how to end an agency relationship with grace.

Chapter 9

Let's Talk about Leaving an Agent

No one likes a bad breakup.

As I have not yet found a husband (if anyone has a son in their mid-to-late twenties, or early thirties, who loves Jesus and loves a career-driven woman ... send them my way), I've experienced quite the harrowing time of dating in today's world.

And having gone out with almost fifty men, (*whew, boy!*), I have enough stories to fill multiple books.

I've been stalked, gaslit, bribed, and told to keep giving them chances.

And as a woman, a very vulnerable woman, I'm sad to say I stayed in some relationships longer than I ought to have because I was scared of the consequences of leaving.

Agency-author agreements can sometimes feel the same way. You've worked so hard to land an agent, and you *really* want to make this work. Try as you might, it ain't working. But leaving the relationship in the wrong way can cause career repercussions.

In this final chapter, we'll discuss the signs that a breakup may be needed and how to make a clean one, while maintaining a good relationship with your former agent and preserving your reputation in the industry.

No one likes to think about this part of the process, but it's best to go in with a strategy, rather than flounder when you reach this point.

Breakup Signs

Feeling tension between yourself and your agent? The first thing you should do is have a conversation with your agent and express your concerns to make sure you fully understand the process. Here are some valid (albeit rare) issues:

- **They Won't Send Your Book Out**

Agents will make sure you have a polished manuscript. And that takes a lot of work. If a manuscript isn't ready to send, then it's to the author's benefit that the agent wait before sending it out.

Also, publishing can go in cycles. There are hard publishing seasons. For example, during 2020-2021, most book projects could not go out.

- **You Disagree on Everything**

You and your agent won't see eye to eye on everything. Maybe they don't send you to your dream house. Maybe they think you need to add a scene to your book you didn't think you needed. Maybe they get you a contract with a house you aren't in love with.

But if you tend to butt heads on everything, you may want to make a clean break with the agent because it's clear you have different and likely incompatible goals

- **They Seem Too Busy for You**

You've sent check-in emails, but they never respond.

Even when they do, they seem to send short messages like, "I have a lot of clients. Have patience."

If you feel they are always too busy for you, then maybe it's time to move on.

- **You Just Feel Ready to Go**

Maybe your agent didn't do anything wrong.

Maybe you're ready to have an agent who does multiple genres, or at least, the genres you want to explore more in-depth. Or you don't want an agent at all and want to explore self-publishing or work with a small press.

Just like with any relationship, authors may have many reasons for why they want to break loose from their agent, some valid and others not as much. How you do end the relationship makes all the difference, though.

How to Break Up with Your Agent

As mentioned before, the very first step in this process should be to have a conversation with your agent. Sometimes the agent is unaware that the author is unhappy enough to consider leaving. Sometimes the author is unaware of what's going on behind the scenes—a death in the family, a chronic illness, a computer meltdown, or that the agent has been held up for a legitimate reason beyond his or her control.

And sometimes, it may be that both the author and agent simply need to improve their communication skills. One tip on communication is to make sure to use "we" or "I" language, never "you" language.

Use wording such as "I need to go in a different direction with my books," or "We had a great run, but I'm being called in a different direction now."

If you feel you had issues with the way the agent handled things, still always give them the benefit of the doubt wherever you can because they were likely doing their best for you.

With this in mind, make sure to take these steps.

First, during the contract stage, make sure they've included a Termination Clause, or some sort of clause that tells you how you can leave the agency. We covered this in a previous chapter, so I won't reiterate much here.

Send them an email about how you've appreciated the time they've invested in your work, but you believe it's time for you to make an exit. Ask how to proceed.

Most agents will abide by this. They don't want their clients to be unhappy.

Finally, ask them how you can help during the severance. Maybe the agent will want the ability to check in with publishers for the next few months before you sign on with another agency to tie up any loose ends.

Be flexible in terms of breaking off the agreement. And show extra gratitude for what they have done.

What Happens if Your Agent Breaks up with You?

This happens too.

At the end of an agreement term, an agent may say, "We had a good run, but I feel our business relationship has run its course."

Or before the end of the agreement, maybe they sense that they can't place your work anywhere. Or maybe they realize that the two of you never really clicked.

Or maybe they're just stepping down from agenting. I had to do this when I accepted a job as an acquisitions editor. I felt like agenting and publishing the same genres served as a conflict of interest, so I had to say goodbye to one role.

If an agent breaks up with you, you can do the following.

First, if you enjoyed your time at the agency, ask if someone else at the agency—a junior agent or associate agent—can adopt your work. Do this with caution and get on a call with the new agent.

Why?

The new agent doesn't know you and may not be as enthusiastic about your work as the first one. After all, they didn't find you in the slush pile. They didn't say, "I choose you from among thousands of submissions."

If you want to work with a different agency altogether, you will have to start the querying process again. Sometimes an agency will refer you to another one, but it's rarer.

During your time at your agency, make as many connections as possible. It never hurts to connect with other agents and publishers while signed at an agency. You never know when a former connection will come in handy.

But Hopefully ...

Hopefully you have a wonderful relationship with your agent, and maybe you don't have to worry about this for years, if ever.

Agents do a lot for us, and I know we blitzed through quite a few things in eight chapters. Although agents may not seem necessary to some authors, they can make sure you have the protection you need and be your biggest source of encouragement.

And good agents will help open those right doors that authors never could on their own.

Wrapping it Up

Agency breakups happen frequently. Maybe you tried your hardest, and you couldn't make it work for the two of you. Likely, your agent did the same. Handle the breakup with kindness, and follow these simple, final, takeaways.

Let's Talk about Leaving an Agent

- **Takeaway One:** If an agent doesn't communicate with you, acts in an unprofessional manner, disagrees on everything with you, or if you just feel like it's time to go … you may be at the stage where a breakup is best.

- **Takeaway Two:** Use "I" language in the breakup, and make sure to thank the agent for all the hard work he or she has done for you. Most agents spend hundreds, if not thousands, of unpaid hours on each client. Even if it doesn't appear to you as though they did so for you, thank them anyway. You may not know the whole story.

- **Takeaway Three:** You can ask your agent to set you up with a successor agent if you enjoyed your experience at the agency, but most authors will re-enter the querying trenches. It helps to make connections before you get to this point, so you don't start at Square One.

Thank you for spending your time with me, and I'm excited to pass you off to Linda as she discusses the next gatekeeper: publishers.

Part Two

Winning the Hearts of Publishers

By Linda Fulkerson

Chapter 10

Introduction to Winning the Hearts of Publishers

Becoming a published author can be one of the most exciting and rewarding events in your life. However, enduring the publication process can be one of the most frightening and frustrating. It is my hope that the tips and tidbits offered in this section can help alleviate your angst and bypass the bafflements.

Before I get into the meat of this section, I'll answer the question I'm asked frequently: "How did you become a publisher?" With the advent of Kindle Direct Publishing and other easily accessible tools, today nearly anyone can publish pretty much anything, so when someone asks me this or a similar question, the querier usually means, "Tell me the story of how your publishing company started."

I'm certain that each traditional publishing house has its own genesis story, but here's mine.

I wrote my first book in 2002, and I did all the things an author seeking traditional publishing is supposed to do. I had the book edited. I sent out query letters. I signed with a reputable agent. My agent offered some excellent guidance on how to strengthen the book. So, I did everything he suggested, and he began submitting my manuscript.

Introduction to Winning the Hearts of Publishers

And I waited. And waited. And waited some more.

After shopping a book for about a year, I got that dreaded phone call. Our agent-author agreement had expired, and he wasn't going to renew it. The publishers he'd submitted to liked the book. It was needed. It was unique. And, most agreed it was well written. But, he said, the question he'd received over and over was, "Who *is* she?"

Because this particular manuscript was a memoir-styled "How to" piece, that question of "Who is she?" was valid. My then-agent made two more suggestions: First, get famous. And then, either resubmit or self-publish.

My first question was, "How does one become famous?" (And I was serious.) He gave me some great tips on how to build an author platform, including becoming a speaker and blogger. (Social media wasn't a thing back then, and blogging was a toddler.) I did my best at the speaker/blogger thing, but the self-publishing statement niggled in the back of my mind.

In 2003, when I published my first book, self-publishing was nothing like it is today. In fact, it was much like traditional publishing, only financed by the author. I went to a lawyer. Formed a corporation. Hired an editor. Hired a graphic designer who did the cover and formatted the interior layout. Found a printer. Did a print run. Built a website. Blogged. Got speaking engagements. Blogged some more. And, I sold the books.

But the most important thing that happened was I learned. A lot. I finally understood why publishing is slow. I'd just gone through most of the steps personally. And, above all, I learned why it's hard to get a manuscript accepted. Publishing has a lot of moving parts. It was a slow, complicated, and expensive process.

A few short years later (in 2007), Amazon launched its Kindle Direct Publishing platform, and everything changed. Publishing on KDP became fast, easy, and cheap.

I wrote a few more books and got bit by the fiction bug. I studied the craft of writing. Learned a lot about self-editing and attended numerous conferences, building my network of friends in the publishing industry.

As one who had "gone through the process" personally, many authors asked me about platform building, author websites, and blogging. I started a blog coach and consulting business somewhere around 2009. In 2011, I was hired as the online editor for a mid-sized daily newspaper in Texas, and in 2013, I returned to my home state of Arkansas and launched a digital services business that focused on helping authors build their platforms. I have since built dozens of author websites.

Fast forward a few years. One of my website and consulting clients was Kathy Cretsinger, owner of Mantle Rock Publishing. I did a lot of projects for Kathy, including editing a few books. She started the company as a means to help debut authors get a foot in the traditional publishing door. Many authors have written great stories, but with the complexity and competition of the industry, many of those stories were gathering dust, waiting for publication. Kathy wanted to help those authors.

As she grew older (she's in her early 80s now), her vision dimmed, and her body rebelled against the long hours. During a phone conversation in April of 2020, she expressed concern for her company. What would happen to her authors if she retired? Or worse, died?

My mother once said everything you do in life gives you the experience you need for where you are now. And I had a lot of experience. I'd self-published the hard way and the easy way. I had a lot of connections in the industry. I had acquired the technical skills necessary for book production. I had editorial experience. I was a graphic designer. At that time, I'd authored nine books. And, I'd learned a fair bit about marketing.

As Kathy continued expressing her concerns, my mind swirled with questions, but the first one that spewed out was, "Is the company for sale?" After a bit of back-and-forth that included consulting our husbands, we agreed upon a price, and within a few

Introduction to Winning the Hearts of Publishers

weeks, I was off to Kentucky, with a Bill of Sale and a Cashier's Check.

Kathy and Jerry gave me some whirlwind "how to be a traditional publisher" training during my visit, and I left with the rights to publish thirteen contracted titles and republish about forty books. I set up an LLC, opened a bank account, got a business license with the state of Arkansas, and built a website. *Boom!* I was a publisher.

But I didn't want to do things halfway. I want to serve authors and glorify God through this company. I've continued to study the industry trends and have received lots of input and advice from other publishers. Two-and-a-half years later, we've grown. At the time of this writing, we have over one hundred titles in print, forty-plus authors, ten freelance editors, three virtual assistants, and multiple imprints. God has blessed us!

As we go through this section of *Getting Past the Gatekeepers*, please understand that publishing processes vary from house to house. Each publishing company will have its own way of doing things. I don't pretend to know all the ins and outs of a huge publishing company, but the basics, including how to get past the gatekeepers, are fairly standard.

Join me as I share how to win the heart of a publisher.

Chapter 11

Understanding the Various Types of Publishers

By understanding what traditional publishers want (and need), your odds of acceptance will be vastly improved. The remainder of the book will go into the wants/needs of traditional publishers in detail. But before we delve into that, I want to cover the various types of publishers: Traditional; Vanity; Indie/Self-publishing; and Hybrid. This chapter will give a brief overview of each.

Traditional Publishing

Traditional publishing is often the first goal of an aspiring author. Traditional publishing houses cover all the expenses of producing a book and offer some assistance in marketing. Plus, there's a certain validation that comes with being traditionally published because so few manuscripts are accepted. In fact, the general consensus among industry professionals is that less than 2 percent of unsolicited manuscripts are accepted by traditional publishers.

Two percent.

According to Children's Book Insider, around 95 percent of

Understanding the Various Types of Publishers

submitted manuscripts are rejected right off the bat. About 5 percent of writers who submit queries and proposals are invited to submit the full manuscript, and somewhere between 1 and 2 percent of those manuscripts will be accepted.

Those are some tough odds, but the purpose of this book is to help you beat those odds. Many would-be-authors submit prematurely—well before the manuscript is ready for prime time. Factor in the investment of time and money to produce the book and promote the author plus the limited number of available publishing slots, and it's easy to see the challenges authors seeking traditional publishing face.

There are four broad categories of traditional publishers:

- Textbook—Also known as "College Publishing." You won't find most books produced by textbook publishers at your local bookstore, but you can find or order them at the bookstore of your local university.
- Scholarly or Academic—This category includes university presses and some not-for-profit publishers associated with museums, etc.
- Reference—In addition to Textbook and Academic publishers, the other non-trade category produces reference works and technical manuals.
- Trade—These are the commercial houses that produce books consumers buy to read for pleasure and, in the case of nonfiction, to learn. For the purpose of this book, we will discuss traditional publishers of Trade books.

Traditional publishers can be divided into three main sizes: Large, mid-sized (often referred to as midsize or midlist), and small. All traditional publishers cover the expense of producing books, and all traditional publishers pay royalties. But that's where the similarities stop.

Large Publishers

Large publishers offer authors an advance toward future royalties. Once the profits clear the advance, additional royalties will be paid. Some pay quarterly, some semi-annually, and some annually. Large publishers almost always require submissions to go through a literary agent.

These companies have a full publishing team and support staff and may conduct business in more than one location. They produce a high volume of titles each year, distributing to brick-and-mortar stores as well as libraries. Large publishers typically do a print run rather than producing books using print-on-demand.

Large publishers have multiple imprints, and some are owned by huge media conglomerates. The publishing industry often refers to the five largest publishing houses as the "Big Five," which includes Simon and Schuster, HarperCollins, Hachette Book Group, Macmillan Publishers, and Penguin Random House.

Midsize publishers

A midsize publisher falls somewhere between the "Big 5" and small, independent presses. The definition of a midsize publisher is hard to nail down, but most sources agree that midsize publishers have at least 250 titles in print with sales between $20 and $50 million.

Midsize publishers will sometimes accept unagented submissions, and many offer an advance. They also normally have more than one imprint and publish a variety of genres.

Small publishers

Small publishers produce fewer books annually than their large and midsize counterparts, and their sales volume is also much lower.

Although some small publishers will work with agents, many will work directly with an author throughout the acquisitions process.

A small press may or may not offer an advance, and if an advance is paid, it will be significantly smaller than that of a large house. Small publishers also are limited in the amount of marketing they provide. Many have a small staff and work primarily through services provided by freelancers.

Vanity Publishing

A vanity press, also known as a "subsidy" publisher, is a publishing company that charges authors for publishing expenses. Some of these publishing houses will publish anything that is submitted to them—often without editorial assistance—which has earned this publishing method a bad reputation (for good reason).

Here's a typical scenario: An author finishes a manuscript and submits it to a publishing house she found online—maybe by clicking an ad. The author submits the manuscript, and in a very short time, the author checks her email and sees a subject line that says, "CONGRATULATIONS!" Filled with excitement, the author clicks on the link and completes a profile on the vanity press's website. Soon, her phone rings, and it's her project manager or mentor or whatever title the company uses.

Unfortunately, many vanity publishers are outright scams, and the excited new author-to-be's project manager is nothing more than a hard-ball sales rep who will attempt to upsell her an expensive, and often useless, marketing package in addition to the book's production fees.

Authors who are desperate to see their work in print are the most likely to fall prey to vanity press scams. The best way to avoid wasting money and time is to educate yourself about your publishing options. That is one of the purposes for this book.

It's true, the publishing process is complex, and if you're new, having a mentor guide you through the process is a must. But there are ways to do this without falling prey to publishing predators.

Things to watch for when investigating a company that seems eager to "help" you publish your book:

- The company requires the author to pay for all fees, sometimes upfront. There are legitimate companies who help authors with the grunt work in publishing—formatting, book cover design, editing, consulting, etc. But these legitimate service providers charge for their work, and most will give you a bid and provide references of past clients.
- The company promises to publish your book on Amazon. Publishing to Amazon for the first time can be a little scary. But if you're not going the traditional publishing route, for whatever reason you've decided, then YOU, the author, should be the one uploading the files—not the vanity press. If your book is uploaded to a vanity press's Amazon account, you will have no control over that book.
- Another warning flag is a reading fee requirement. No traditional publishing house will ask you to pay for reading your manuscript. They have acquisitions editors who do that at no cost to the author.
- Other "services" vanity presses sometimes offer are acquiring an ISBN and/or barcode. These items are, of course, provided by a traditional publishing house. But you can buy these on your own if you're planning to self-publish.

Independent ("Indie") and/or Self-Publishing

Originally, Indie or Independent Publishing referred to the process of publishing through a press that was *independently owned* rather than belonging to a large conglomerate or multinational corporation. For years, small presses and niche publishers were called "indie" presses or publishers. And some industry professionals still use the term Indie Publisher when referring to a small independent press.

In recent years, however, the term "Indie" has become synonymous with self-publishing, because self-publishing is the act of producing a book *independently* from any established publishing house.

To avoid confusion, during this section of the book I will use the term "small press" when referring to small, independent traditional publishers, and "self-publishing" when referring to the process of, well, self-publishing.

In self-publishing, the author controls and funds the entire process: cover design, interior layout, editing, formatting, arranging distribution, and marketing.

Hybrid Publishing

This is another term with multiple uses. A hybrid publisher assists authors (for a fee) with the publishing process. Yet it's become commonplace for authors to refer to themselves as "hybrid" if they have books both traditionally and self-published. For the purpose of this section, if I use the word "hybrid," I am referring to the publishing model where authors pay for services rendered during the publishing process, not the "hybrid author" meaning.

One frequently asked question is, "What's the difference between vanity publishing and hybrid publishing?" That's a valid question, because in both publishing models, the author foots the bill. As one who has been in the self-publishing assistance side of the industry for many years, I think the main difference is mission. Vanity presses have the reputation of being mostly after the money, whereas hybrid publishers provide publishing services to authors to help them. True, they don't work for free. But they charge for their time and technical skill. They are service providers—not scam artists.

Vanity publishers have a reputation for using aggressive sales tactics and producing poor-quality products. They also often include hidden fees and upsell useless marketing services. Because so many authors were being taken advantage of by supposed "hybrid" publishers, in February 2018, the Independent Book Publishers Association set forth a list of nine criteria to define what constitutes a legitimate hybrid publisher.

- Define a mission and vision for its publishing program.
- Vet submissions.
- Publish under its own imprint(s) and ISBNs.
- Publish to industry standards
- Ensure editorial, design, and production quality.
- Pursue and manage a range of publishing rights.
- Provide distribution services.
- Demonstrate respectable sales.
- Pay authors a higher-than-standard royalty.

You can read the expanded version and download a printable PDF of this list at the IBPA's website by visiting this link: https://www.ibpa-online.org/page/hybrid-publisher-criteria-download.

Wrapping it Up

As you can see from the information in this chapter, authors have many publication paths to choose from.

- **Takeaway One:** Traditional publishing houses cover all the expenses of producing a book and offer some assistance in marketing. In self-publishing, the author controls and funds the entire process: cover design, interior layout, editing, formatting, arranging distribution, and marketing.

Understanding the Various Types of Publishers

- **Takeaway Two:** There's a difference between hybrid publishers and vanity presses. Make sure you do your research and don't get scammed.

- **Takeaway Three:** Less than 2 percent of unsolicited manuscripts are accepted by traditional publishers. By learning how to win the hearts of a traditional publisher, you can beat the odds.

Chapter 12

Understanding What Publishers Want

Winning the heart of a publisher boils down to understanding and providing what they want.

Ultimately, what publishers want is a great story for their fiction readers and a valuable resource for nonfiction readers. However, that story or resource must be marketable, because if a publisher can't sell enough copies to make the book financially viable, it will be rejected no matter how great your idea is.

Sometimes it's hard to calculate whether or not a book will make a profit, but there are certain criteria publishers consider when reviewing a proposal.

The Author

When you submit a manuscript to a publisher, whether it goes through an acquisitions editor at a larger house or is received directly by the owner of a small press, the publisher will research you.

Questions that go through my mind when I receive a new manuscript are:

- **Is the author professional?** Professionalism includes everything from your online presence—website, social media profiles, even your email address—to how well you followed the submission guidelines and formatted your proposal.
- **Does the author have plans to write more books?** When you submit your proposal, include ideas (or blurbs, if you have them) for future projects. If no specific projects are in the works, at the very least state that you intend to write more books (if you do). Publishers invest time and resources developing in new authors. If you only want to have one title published, traditional publishing is probably not your best option. Publishers don't have the time or money to invest in one-hit wonders.
- **Is the author well-read?** Writing is a lot like playing chess. If you only compete against those at the same or lower skill level as you, it will be very difficult to improve. Read in your desired genre. Read outside your genre. Read new releases. Read classics. And learn from what you read. "Don't read a book and be a follower; read a book and be a student." — Jim Rohn
- **Does the author have the credentials to write this book?** If you've been around the writing community for any length of time, you've probably heard, "Write what you know." Writing from experience makes an author's words ring true. If you're a nonfiction author, then credentials are vital to the success of a book.
- **Does the author have a platform?** The chapter on book marketing will cover this in more detail, but it's very disappointing to receive a proposal that I'm interested in only to learn that the author hasn't even tried to start building a platform. Some don't even have a website. I have actually heard an aspiring author say, "I

didn't want to go to the expense and effort of a website until I know my book will be published." Those two words—expense and effort—are what most publishing professionals would consider an investment in the author's writing career. If you want to win the heart of a publisher, get an author website, start building your email list, and work on growing a social media presence. If you're new, publishers get it. We work with debut authors frequently. But if you haven't even begun to build a platform, you'll likely get a hard pass from most publishers.

- **Is the author easy to work with?** I've had friends in the industry discuss debut authors who had a diva complex and expected publishing professionals to cater to their whims even though they'd never been published. Be friendly. Kind. Considerate. Those actions will gain you points. Being rude, impatient, and demanding will get you rejected.

The Manuscript

Many authors hire a freelance editor to help prepare the manuscript for consideration. While this step isn't necessary, it's a good idea if you have the budget for it. If you can't afford a full-fledged edit, go for a paid critique by someone who edits your genre. Then, take his or her suggestions and go through the manuscript. Look for similar issues and correct those before you send your proposal.

Perhaps you have certain filter words that creep into your writing, or you're fond of prepositional phrases, or you've overused pronouns. Things like this can be overlooked by the one who wrote the piece, but another set of eyes can spot things that the author missed. Don't let that first set of extra eyes be the acquisitions editor or publisher.

When I'm reading a submission, I'm always looking for a great story. But the underlying question in my mind is, "Can this person write well?"

I recently received a query that was so intriguing, I requested that the author submit the full manuscript with the proposal. I'm sure she was thrilled at the prospect, but after reading the first page, I saw at least a dozen serious issues with her writing ability. Unfortunately, we had to pass on that submission.

Soon afterward, I requested the full manuscript from another author. The story was so good, I breezed through the manuscript in two days, mentally noting areas that needed to be fixed while I read. (Sorry, that's how editors think.) There were less than five noticeable issues in a 90,000-word manuscript. We offered that author a contract. A few more errors may surface during the editorial process, but her manuscript was polished and ready to submit. It was a joy to read.

Make sure your manuscript is formatted correctly. Check with the submission guidelines and see if there are instructions on formatting. If not, use standard manuscript formatting. For the layout, use 1-inch margins all around. On the Paragraph tab of Microsoft Word, make sure the alignment is left, and set the indentation to special > first line by 0.5". Do not tab to indent paragraphs. Double space your manuscript with 0 pt. spacing before and after paragraphs. For scene breaks, use three hashtags, centered, with extra lines before or after them. Submitting a properly formatted manuscript is a great way to win the heart of a potential publisher.

The Platform

Is platform really a big deal? The short answer is yes.

One reason platform is important is because a large platform helps with the initial book launch. For instance, when a new release hits the top tier on Amazon, that title gets bonus exposure from Amazon—for free. Sometimes that exposure comes in the form of

Getting Past the Publishing Gatekeepers

being placed in the "Books you may like," "Explore similar books," and "Related to items you've viewed" sections. Books are placed in some areas of Amazon's website because of ads, such as the ones with the word "Sponsored" displayed above the row of covers, but Amazon's algorithm places unsponsored books in high profile places as well. Then there's the coveted #1 Best Seller banner. That's a perk that would make any author proud.

Things publishers look for as far as platform include a popular blog (oh, yes, blogging is still a thing—an important one!); email newsletter list; speaking engagements; podcasts; radio or television shows; and social media presence. And having previously published books that have done well is another part of an author's platform.

It's never too early to start building an author platform. And there are two keys to doing so: be consistent and be persistent.

Wrapping it Up

Ultimately, what publishers want is a great story for their fiction readers and a valuable resource for nonfiction readers. However, that story or resource must be marketable, because if a publisher can't sell enough copies to make the book financially viable, it will be rejected no matter how great your idea is.

- **Takeaway One:** Publishers expect authors to invest in their writing career. This will take time, money, and effort.

- **Takeaway Two:** Make sure your manuscript is polished, formatted correctly, and ready to submit.

- **Takeaway Three:** It's never too early to start building an author platform.

Chapter 13

Understanding What Publishers Do (And Don't Do)

What do publishers do?

The short answer is, of course, publishers produce books. But publishers do much more than that. A publisher is, in effect, a project manager that oversees the entire process of selecting manuscripts with viable sales potential, development of author careers, book production (details about the publishing process will be discussed in another chapter), sales and promotion, product distribution, and disbursement of royalties and other business management tasks.

The purpose of this chapter is to give you a quick overview of the tasks involved in publishing. Several of these tasks will be detailed in subsequent chapters.

Manuscript Acquisitions

I've devoted an entire chapter to the acquisition process, and Rowena covered this in the Editor section of this book as well. It may seem redundant to go into such detail about one topic, but this part of the process is where the magic happens. It's where the author takes that first step to reach out and submit his or her manuscript to a publishing professional. It's where the publisher gets a twinge of excitement, wondering, "Will this be the one?"

Author Career Development

Although many aspects of publishing are standard, developing author careers varies greatly from house to house. Not only does the development process of an author's career vary, defining the term itself is open for debate.

Some publishers believe it's the author's responsibility to develop his or her career. It is. But, it's also to the publisher's advantage to invest in authors. All good business owners know it's easier to nurture and retain a customer than it is to acquire a new one. When a publisher acquires a good author, it's best to help him or her grow in both the writing craft and building his or her platform. See the chapter on author responsibilities for more about the author's part in this process.

Book Production

This is the heart and soul of what publishers do. Book production is (literally) the company's bread and butter. Another chapter will go into detail about the publishing process.

Manage Distribution

I use the word "manage" here, because most book publishers don't actually distribute the books. The majority of publishers use book distributors, which either print books on demand, warehouse stock for print runs, drop-ship author and publisher copies, and handle the order fulfillments, whether it be to booksellers or directly to customers.

Marketing and Promotion

It goes without saying that marketing is a big part of the publishing industry. Many people confuse the words "marketing" and "sales." They are not the same thing. This is another topic to which I've devoted an entire chapter.

Accounting and Business Management

This area is part of any business—large or small—but it is one of the duties of a publisher, so I've included it here. Each house handles things differently, but things such as sales reports, royalty statements and disbursements, and tax forms and payments are all part of the publisher's responsibilities.

Customer Service

A good bit of my time as a small press owner is spent responding to questions and "directing traffic." Larger companies have entire departments dedicated to this area, but as is the case with many small presses, most queries come directly to me. Our company has freelance editors and virtual assistants, but our company's email goes straight to my inbox.

Our authors can also contact me personally when they have questions, issues, or just need advice on how to approach an area of their story. Plus, we receive emails and contact form submissions from readers, agents, reviewers, author publicists, etc. This is one of those behind-the-scenes parts of publishing that can be both rewarding and time-consuming. But it is one of the things publishers do.

What do (most) publishers NOT do?

You can see from the above list that publishers do a lot of things.

Understanding What Publishers Do (And Don't Do)

Book planning and production is a complex process. I have a project management system that includes over seventy tasks for the production of each title. But even with all the things publishers *do*, there are many things that most publishers *don't* do.

Print books

Many readers are surprised to learn that few publishers actually print the books they publish. Printing is almost always outsourced. Publishers are busy acquiring new titles, editing, designing, and promoting books and authors. Book printing technology changes frequently, so it's easier and more cost effective for publishers to pay for print runs or use a print-on-demand service.

Distribute books

For the most part, publishers partner with a book wholesaler or distribution service. Some printers offer such services, but the majority of books are distributed by a handful of wholesalers. Ingram is the largest book supplier to bookstores and other retailers, and Baker & Taylor is the largest distributor to libraries.

Direct book sales

While larger publishers may warehouse titles and sell directly to the consumer, most small presses don't need the added expense of purchasing large quantities of books, not to mention storage space and costs as well as the time and resources necessary to maintain an online store. A lot of small publishing companies have limited office space and most use freelance services in lieu of employees. It's quicker, easier, and cheaper to use another service to process the payments and fulfill orders.

Wrapping it Up

Publishers produce books, but they do much more than that.

- **Takeaway One:** The acquisitions part of the process is where the magic happens. It's where the publisher gets a twinge of excitement, wondering, "Will this be the one?"

- **Takeaway Two:** Some publishers believe it's the author's responsibility to develop his or her career. It is. But, it's also to the publisher's advantage to invest in authors.

- **Takeaway Three:** Many people confuse the words "marketing" and "sales." They are not the same thing.

Chapter 14

Understand that Publishing is a Business

Writers are creatives. Artists. Free spirits. Publishers are business people. Entrepreneurs. Number crunchers.

Imagine a balding man in the corner office clenching his teeth around a half-smoked cigar. Suspenders and a bow tie contrast against the shirt he's wearing—the one with buttons straining against the flesh they've been tasked to contain. Glasses perched on the edge of his nose, he peers over them as you enter the room holding your manuscript. He isn't smiling.

That's a virtual scenario of what it looks like when a submission form notification pops into a small publisher's email account. He or she may *want* to be excited about the possibility of acquiring a new story, but chances are that this one, like so many before it, doesn't have the marketing potential to warrant publication consideration.

Traditional publishing houses must make a profit in order to operate, therefore not all books will be accepted. In fact, most books won't. Many factors go into the decision of whether or not to offer a publishing contract. And sometimes, it's not the writing that has the publisher's hands hovering over the keyboard, poised to peck out a

Understand that Publishing is a Business

rejection message. It's often the timing. Because the publishing industry operates on trends.

As you're working to polish your manuscript and prepare your proposal, remember that in publishing, the hours are long and the margins are thin. Watch for trends in the market. See what is selling and what isn't. There's a definite ebb and flow.

For example, for several years, Chick Lit was a popular genre. I had an idea for a Chick Lit mystery novel. But by the time I got around to writing it, that trend had passed. True, there are still some books published in that genre, but it isn't at the top of a publisher's must-have list.

Look at Amazon's Hot New Releases list. See which genres are topping that list. Read the reviews and see what readers want. Yes, you need to write the book you wish to write, but if your particular genre isn't selling well at this time, you may have to wait. Or be rejected. Or self-publish.

One thing to remember, though. Publishers are looking for great stories. Make yours the best you can, and who knows, that crusty balding publisher in the back corner office may just pick up the phone and call you.

Wrapping it Up

Writers are creatives, but publishers are businesspeople.

- **Takeaway One:** A publisher may *want* to be excited about the possibility of acquiring a new story, but if it doesn't have the marketing potential to warrant publication consideration it will be rejected.

- **Takeaway Two:** Many factors go into the decision of whether or not to offer a publishing contract. And sometimes, it's not the writing that prompts a rejection.

- **Takeaway Three:** Write the book you wish to write, but if your particular genre isn't selling well at this time, you may have to wait. Or be rejected. Or self-publish.

Chapter 15

Understanding the Acquisitions Process

You've written a great book and polished your manuscript. Now, it's time to get your book published. This is the point where aspiring authors encounter the gatekeepers. I've said many times that there's more to writing a book than writing a book. Without discounting the hard work that goes into that process, sometimes it's the easy part.

But we're here to help you get past those pesky gatekeepers so you can enter the wonderful world of published authors. In order to win the heart of publishers, it's helpful to understand the acquisitions process.

Do your research

I once worked as an office manager, and one of my duties was assisting with screening job applicants. As résumés rolled in, the first thing I did was sort them into two piles: Those who met the job qualifications and those who didn't. The submissions in the "didn't" pile would soon be issued a "thanks, but no thanks" letter. Taking a

Understanding the Acquisitions Process

few minutes to read the blurb about what we were looking for would have saved our office a lot of time.

The same principle applies to proposal submissions. Read what the publisher publishes. It's always a plus when the cover letter includes a sentence such as, "I read the book [insert title] recently published by your company, and I believe my story is comparable." This tells me that the author has invested some time to research the type of books we publish and determined that his or her book may be a good fit.

At this point, instead of sending off a standard thanks-for-thinking-of-us-but-this-proposal-doesn't-fit-our-editorial-needs response, I'm going to freshen my coffee and take a few minutes to browse through the proposal. If the concept and the writing are good, I'll request the full manuscript.

The author doesn't have to take the time to read a whole book, but it's nice. Just knowing he or she has browsed through our website, found a book or two that is similar in genre and concept, and complied with the submissions guidelines is a huge improvement over many submissions we receive.

A few minutes of research can go a long way toward winning a publisher's heart.

Build your platform

When I receive a proposal, after ensuring the author has researched our guidelines, one of the next things I do is Google the author's name. If he has a good Internet presence, I continue to the next step of the acquisitions process.

Publishers make money by selling books. Book marketing is hard. Consumers have a lot of choices on where to spend their disposable income. So, it's vital for authors to work on building their platform so readers can know they exist.

A platform enables one to be seen above the crowd—it's a stage, of sorts. If you've ever been to a concert, think back to how tiny the artist appeared from the arena's nosebleed section. If you squint hard enough, you may be able to make out a few facial features, but it's difficult.

There are a few ways to boost the visibility of the performer. You can zoom in with your phone's camera and snap a photo, but with poor lighting, it's likely to be blurred. Some concert producers place large-screen TVs at key points in the building. That's helpful—if one isn't blocking your view. But one of the best ways is to bring a pair of high-power binoculars. Now you can see clearly as if the singer were right in front of you. Binoculars are great tools for boosting the visibility of something or someone far away.

An author platform works the same way. A reader may have heard of you, but you need to be directly in her focal point to get her attention. When someone searches the Internet for a specific type of book, your books need to display in the search results, preferably on the first page. This takes time and effort, but it's key to getting the attention of a publisher.

Get an Agent (or not)

If you wish to be published with a large publishing house, you must first get an agent. If you wish to work with a small publisher, many times it's not necessary. Again, you can learn the requirements of your desired publisher by checking the guidelines on their website.

Craft a book proposal

Think of your book proposal as a résumé for your dream job, but the main purpose of the proposal is to entice the agent, editor, or publisher to ask for the full manuscript.

You can find a lot of advice by searching online for what to include in a book proposal. But basically, it comes down to three questions: (1) Why does the world need this book? (2) Who would read it? and (3) What qualifies you to write it?

Understanding the Acquisitions Process

If the publisher's submissions guidelines don't specify exactly what they want in the proposal, the essential elements are: an introductory letter that includes the book's hook; a short synopsis of the book; and sample chapters, typically two or three.

It's also recommended to include some comparable titles, explaining what makes your book unique. Add an "about the author" section that includes details about your platform. If your book is fiction, you may also include brief sketches of the main characters, including their goal, motivation, conflict, and stakes.

Write a great query letter

For publishers who have asked aspiring authors to "query first," you'll need to start with a query letter before sending the proposal. Even if you submit a proposal, you'll need a cover letter, which should include the same information as a query.

The query should be no more than one page, single-spaced. After the greeting, you may add a short opening, especially if you met the publisher, agent, or editor in person at a conference.

Make sure your query letter includes the book's basic information: genre and sub-genre (for fiction) and/or topic (for nonfiction); approximate word count; and, of course, the title and subtitle. For fiction, if this title is intended to launch a series, state that as well.

Next comes the hook. Think: back cover copy. This hook is what will entice readers to buy the book, but it should also pique the interest of the publisher enough to request a full manuscript. The hook should be brief but will also comprise the bulk of your letter. Somewhere between 150-300 words is a good guideline for the letter's hook. Some queries open with the hook, followed by the book's basics. That format is also fine.

What should you include in the hook? Think character's goals, motivation, conflict, and stakes. Who is your protagonist? What is their main problem? What does that character want and why? What or who will get in the way of them attaining that goal? What choices do they need to make?

For nonfiction, write a compelling description of your book's narrative. Include the target audience. Who would benefit from reading this book and why?

Before closing, include a very brief bio—no less than a hundred words. Focus on any credentials that qualify you to write this book. (Credentials are especially important for nonfiction.) End by thanking the person for his or her time.

Wait

When my daughter was around two years old, we used to sing a song that went something like this, "Have patience. Have patience. Don't be in such a hurry ..." Patience is hard for toddlers. It's also hard for a writer waiting to hear back after submitting a query letter or proposal.

Please understand that publishing professionals are typically overworked. For small publishing houses with limited staff, working on the books in progress takes precedence over slogging through the slush pile. And larger companies may have multiple acquisitions editors. Both small and large houses have a pub board that reviews proposals and manuscripts recommended by the acquisitions editors. It's a long process.

But know that just as a Top 25 football coach spends a good deal of time recruiting new talent, screening submissions is vital to the company's success, so someone *will* get to it. Hopefully soon.

Check the company's website. There may be an estimation of how long the submission review process takes. If there isn't a "no contact" request on their site, and the review timeframe has passed, it's fine to send a brief follow-up email and request an update on the status of your submission. But understand that not all publishing houses respond to queries. In some cases, no response means your submission wasn't accepted.

Understanding the Acquisitions Process

Accept rejections

Unfortunately, rejections are often part of the submission process. This book's purpose is to help writers get past the gatekeepers by teaching how to improve the areas you have control over—write a great book, research before you submit, build your author platform, be as professional as possible, etc.

But there are some things beyond your control. Writing is subjective. Perhaps what you and your critique partners thought was awesome didn't strike a chord with the first reader at the publishing house. Maybe their editorial calendar is full for that particular genre. Maybe they just published (or have scheduled) something similar to your story.

The key to getting published is to keep working on your craft. Keep building your platform. Keep polishing your proposal. And keep submitting. Persistence wins. Remember: "A river cuts through rock, not because of its power, but because of its persistence." ~ Jim Watkins

Polish your manuscript

While you're submitting and waiting, you can form an army of beta readers, preferably those who have an excellent grasp of story and grammar, and request that they give your manuscript a good read-through.

Wait? Won't the publishing company edit the manuscript? Yes. But it never hurts to have it as perfect as possible when you turn your manuscript in.

And, when your manuscript is accepted for publication, you can then turn to these readers and invite them to join your street team and/or write reviews when your book is published.

Official Acceptance

As you continue polishing, submitting, and waiting, the time will come when you'll receive an official acceptance. Sometimes this is "the call," when an acquisitions editor or agent or small press owner picks up the phone and offers to publish your book. Sometimes the official offer is sent via email. It's an exciting moment, often filled with squeals of joy.

At this point, you have a few options. If you know this is the publisher you want to work with, then you can accept the offer and sign the contract that will follow. If you are unsure or if you are interested but have questions, it's fine to ask for time to think. Remember, though, that publication slots fill quickly, so don't ask for too much time. Maybe a couple of weeks.

During this time, you may wish to request that some of the authors who have been published with this company contact you so you can see how they like working with this publisher. You may also ask to review a copy of the contract, but know that debut authors and authors without a long successful track record will likely receive the company's standard contract and may not be able to negotiate.

The Contract

I'm not going to offer legal advice here, but read through the contract before you sign and submit it. If there is anything in it you don't understand and you don't have an agent, you can request to discuss it with the publisher.

Most publishing contracts have similar elements—Grant of Rights (and what rights are being granted to the publisher); Territory (where the books will be distributed); Whether or not an advance is offered; Royalties (amounts and frequency of disbursements); Subsidiary Rights (secondary rights the publisher may license to other entities, and how those sales will be split); Manuscript Delivery and Acceptance (your submission deadlines and what the publisher expects from the manuscript—word count, delivery method, etc.); and Reversion of Rights (including what constitutes "out of print").

If your book will be produced using digital and/or print-on-demand technology, then the "out of print" clauses may specify low revenue criteria that would place the book in an "out of print" status.

Other elements may be included in book publishing contracts, but these are some of the essentials. If anything about the contract looks weird or "fishy," consult a legal professional and have it reviewed. Our company has had our standard contract reviewed by two attorneys and several literary agents to ensure we are in line with industry standards and that the language is clear.

Write, Self-edit, and Revise

Your publisher may include a manuscript submission checklist or an email specifying exactly how the manuscript should be formatted and house-specific stylistic preferences. You will have some time between the contract signing and the manuscript due date to make sure your manuscript is as polished as possible before turning it in.

If you turn in a manuscript that is basically a first draft and requires what I call a "hard edit," your publisher may have the right to reject it or reschedule it, depending on the contract wording. Authors who submit manuscripts that aren't publishable will not win the hearts of their publishers. Those authors may have received a contract, but they may not receive another one.

Nonfiction authors will sometimes receive a contract based upon the proposal and sample chapters, even if the book isn't finished. And fiction authors who have a track record with the publisher may also receive a contract for unfinished works. Your publisher will likely ask how long you need to complete the project and reflect that time when the manuscript due date is set in your contract.

Wrapping it Up

The acquisitions process is the point where aspiring authors encounter the gatekeepers.

- **Takeaway One:** Invest some time to research the type of books the publisher you're pitching to publishes and determined whether or not your book would be a good fit.

- **Takeaway Two:** Consumers have a lot of choices on where to spend their disposable income. So, it's vital for authors to work on building their platform so readers can know they exist.

- **Takeaway Three:** Understand that debut authors and authors without a long successful track record will likely receive the company's standard contract and may not be able to negotiate.

Chapter 16

Understand the Publishing Process

Many first-time authors are surprised when they receive an acceptance letter only to discover the release date for their book is two (or more) years away. Traditional publishing takes time.

So, what takes publishers so long to produce a book?

After the acquisitions process, which was explained in a separate chapter, the manuscript enters the editorial and publishing process. While each publishing house will have its own system, book publishing requires several complex steps.

Pre-publication Planning

As soon as the manuscript is officially accepted for publication, the publisher launches the book's publishing project. I use a project management system to keep me on track of each book's progress. I'm sure each publishing house has its own workflow, but here's a list of tasks I perform before the actual editing begins:

- Schedule the book on the editorial spreadsheet. My spreadsheet has columns for the book's major information

as well as deadlines for each part of the process. It currently has separate worksheets for three years in advance.
- Editors are then assigned to the manuscript and listed on the spreadsheet.
- Contracts for the author and editors are issued. We use freelance editors, and therefore need a contract for each project. For larger companies, which hire editors as employees, no editorial contracts are needed.
- When the contract is issued, we also send the author a cover design worksheet, a copy of our company's policies and procedures, and a manuscript submissions checklist.
- Create a digital file folder for the book. I place each book folder within a folder by year and begin each book folder's title with the scheduled release date so I can see at a glance the entire year of books in order. Everything associated with that book project is saved in this folder. At the end of the year, I archive the year's folder to an external hard drive.
- If the author is new, then we set up an author file in our customer relationship management (CRM) database, add the author to our website, and create a folder with the author's headshot and bio.
- New authors are then added to our private Facebook group, which is used for communication, announcements, and networking. We also have a sub-website for the author portal, which is where sales reports are posted, so I set up a user account for the new author there as well.
- The publisher also assigns an ISBN (International Standard Book Number) through their Bowker account. An ISBN is unique to each edition of the title, so if the title is to be released in eBook, paperback, hardcover, and audiobook, four ISBNs will be assigned.

Getting Past the Publishing Gatekeepers

- A request is submitted to the Library of Congress for an LCCN (Library of Congress Control Number).

First Read

Larger houses may employ first readers. For smaller presses, this is often done by either the owner or one of the acquisitions editors. During the first read-through, manuscript issues that need to be addressed by the developmental editor are noted. Perhaps the story is great and the writing is good, but the ending is contrived or rushed. Maybe a subplot has been left unresolved.

After the first read, the manuscript enters the editorial process. Again, different publishing houses have different systems, but I'm going to share a brief overview of the editorial process. Rowena will go more in-depth about what each editor looks for in her section of this book.

Developmental Edit

The developmental, also known as content edit, is big picture editing. A content editor looks for plot holes, character arcs, structure, etc., and makes sure the entire story is cohesive. This edit is primarily used for fiction, although nonfiction does need to have good structure and flow, as well.

A developmental editor may require extensive revisions in the manuscript, and typically, at least for fiction, this is the longest segment of the editorial process.

Line Edit

Line edits are often confused with the copy edit. A line edit is a detailed look at the story—scene by scene, paragraph by paragraph, line by line. Line editors also perform fact checks, fix sentence syntax issues, and more. Again, the line editing process takes some time to make everything as correct as possible.

Copy Edit

Some line editors perform a copy edit simultaneously with the line edit. A copy edit takes care of problems found in punctuation, grammar, spelling, and word usage.

Proofreading

The last stage of the editorial process for most publishing companies is the final proofread. At this point, the book is read out loud. In my company, I request that not only one of the editorial staff proof the book but that the author performs this step as well. Even though at this point the manuscript has been polished by the author before submission and seen by at least two or three editors, mistakes are still found.

Formatting

The next step in the publishing process is formatting the manuscript into a file usable for printing (for paperback and hardcover editions) and digital distribution (for eBook editions).

There are many formatting software programs available to aid the publisher in doing this. Even Microsoft Word can be used, and I've done it, but there are much easier ways. Many publishers use Adobe InDesign for the interior design, which allows for a lot of control over how the book will look. Vellum (Mac only) and Atticus simplify the formatting process but use pre-set format options, which limits the appearance of the final product.

Corrections

Corrections found during the final proof are made either to the manuscript's document or, if the formatted galley has been used for the final proof (which is how we do it so formatting issues can also be identified), then those corrections are edited directly using the formatting program.

Design

Design includes both the cover as well as the interior layout of the book. Many choices are made in the design process, from images to font pairings. Some publishing companies allow little input from the author on the cover design, but some have the authors complete a cover design worksheet of some sort. For others, including ours, the author has a lot of say in the cover design process, but the ultimate decision is that of the publisher.

The book cover design process usually begins around the same time as the editorial process so book covers can be revealed in marketing pieces long before the book is published.

Publishing

Once the book is properly formatted, the publisher uploads the files to a distributor's publishing platform for print-on-demand titles, or to the printer, if the book will have a print run. Some publishers use multiple publishing methods.

For small publishers, the most popular publishing platforms are Amazon and IngramSpark. Both platforms enable the publisher to produce paperback, hardcover, and eBook editions of the book.

For books produced by a print-on-demand company, the publisher completes the metadata information during the process of uploading the files. The metadata is all relevant information about

Understand the Publishing Process

the book—title, subtitle, ISBN, price, publication date, description, age-appropriateness, categories, keywords, etc.

Publishers research keywords and categories to ensure proper placement of the book and to make it easier for potential readers to find.

Managing Printing and Distribution

As mentioned elsewhere in this section, most publishers don't print or distribute their own books. However, they do manage the outsourcing of printing and distribution and ensure those processes go smoothly.

When the books are ready to order, the publisher then orders promotional copies for authors and/or others (editors, agents, etc.), according to the terms of their contract.

Promotion

Finally, the book is done! But promotion has begun long before this point. The publisher and author have both taken many steps to ensure that potential readers are aware of the newly released title. These can include advertisements, book trailers, printed material, blog tours, social media campaigns, launch parties, pre-order promotions, contests, free chapter previews, email announcements, and more.

Promotion is a partnership between the author and the publisher. And part of winning the heart of a publisher is being willing to take part in promoting your book. It's a fun and exciting step in the publishing process!

Wrapping it Up

Traditional publishing takes time, and understanding the process

Getting Past the Publishing Gatekeepers

can help you win the heart of a publisher through your demonstrated patience, flexibility, and preparedness

- **Takeaway One:** A developmental editor may require extensive revisions in the manuscript, and typically, at least for fiction, this is the longest segment of the editorial process.

- **Takeaway Two:** A line edit is a detailed look at the story—scene by scene, paragraph by paragraph, line by line.

- **Takeaway Three:** Some publishing companies allow little input from the author on the cover design and others allow a lot of say in the cover design process. But the ultimate decision is that of the publisher.

Chapter 17

Understand the Basics of Book Marketing

This book isn't about marketing, *per se*, but because understanding book marketing basics can help you win the heart of a publisher, this chapter will give a brief overview of book marketing and offer some tips used by bestselling authors.

The first thing to understand is that marketing and selling are not the same. Marketing can lead to sales, but it also boosts brand awareness (and if you're an author, *you* are the brand) and builds trust in your readers.

Digital marketers often call this effect of marketing the "Know-Like-Trust" system. The KLT system basically goes like this: The more people get to know you, the more they will like you. The more they like you, the more likely they are to buy your products.

The next thing to understand is that while social media has its place in the author's marketing toolbox, it is not your most powerful tool. In this chapter, I'll share with you the secret used by bestselling authors.

Have you ever wondered why some authors sell thousands of copies of their books but others sell just a few? Let's compare a book launch campaign of an average author to that of a bestselling author.

Understand the Basics of Book Marketing

Average Author's Book Launch Campaign

- Build an online community of social media followers
- Promote book via social media
- Ask their fellow author friends to write reviews. If they are published traditionally, the publisher may send out advanced reader copies (either digitally or hard copies)
- Set up a blog tour
- Schedule a book signing
- Possibly hire a publicist to submit press releases and set up interviews
- Post about the new book on their blog
- And, when they write another book, repeat the process

There's actually nothing wrong with any of the above items. In fact, I recommend most of those actions to our authors. But there's a missing step, and that step is vital to a book's success. It's what makes the difference between mediocre sales and bestselling status.

Bestselling Author's Book Launch Campaign

- Build an effective email marketing list
- Send an email to that list

If you're thinking, "But I *did* send out an email to my list!" Then that's great! The difference between your results and the bestselling author's is one word: *effective*. If your email list isn't effective, it won't be useful to you.

It's been my experience that growing and nurturing an effective email list is the best way to increase your book sales. And marketing experts agree.

"If there's one thing all professional platform-builders agree on, it's the importance of building your list." —Michael Hyatt

"While social media and networking are great ways to connect and build relationships, they are not the most effective sales tools. Statistics have proven that an active email-marketing list outperforms social media marketing 14:1." —Social Triggers

The best thing about building an email list is that it can be done long before your book is published. In fact, it should be.

What is the goal of marketing, really?

In a nutshell, the purpose of marketing is to reach the right person with the right message at the right time.

Who is the right person?

Someone who reads the type of writing you produce. This group of persons is called your target audience. The best part about email list members is that they have *chosen* to join your online community. They actually *want* to hear from you.

What is the right message?

If you've worked hard to grow an email list and only send out messages whenever you have a new book release, then your list won't be effective. In fact, many will unsubscribe. You'll need to *nurture* that list of subscribers so they will remember who you are when you have a book release. So, you'll need to send out emails frequently enough to keep your name familiar, but not so often that you annoy them.

The frequency itself isn't as much an issue as the content you send. Because if you're sending something they *want* to read, they'll actually look forward to receiving your emails. There are two words to keep in mind when contacting your list: relevant and useful.

When you send out a message, keep it simple. Be personable. And remember this: it's not about you, but how you can *help* your readers. Other than Uncle Charlie and Grandma Sue, most of your subscribers don't care about you (sorry).

People in general are selfish. They likely subscribed to your list in the first place to get something free. And the only thing that will keep them on the list (and keep them happy and interested) is to respond to their WIIFM (What's in it for me?) thinking.

The right message is anything that is useful and relevant to your target audience. Keep your content interesting. Entertaining. Enlightening. Become a sharer of cool things.

What is the right time?

The right time is whenever it's convenient for your audience. When they will be receptive to consuming your content.

This is one reason advertising isn't as effective as it once was. Unless a potential consumer sees an ad at the exact moment he or she has a need that ad can fill, they will likely forget about it. (For example, have you ever seen an ad for a dental clinic while you're zipping down the Interstate at 70 mph? Unless you're experiencing tooth pain at that moment, will you even care about that billboard?)

One of the best benefits about content marketing, especially through email, is that your message is delivered at your convenience but received at your audience's. Email can be read when the reader is ready. It doesn't disrupt their day like a telemarketer. It isn't missed, which is what happens to the vast majority of social media marketing posts.

Now that social platforms are moving more and more toward boosting paid content and diminishing organic posts, having your message noticed is challenging. Consider this: the average "lifespan" of a tweet is just a few minutes.

Why focus on email?

Because people *want* to hear from email list owners.

Getting Past the Publishing Gatekeepers

As I mentioned earlier, your list members have chosen to be there. They signed up. They *expect* to receive messages from you. And, according to the following quote from Marketing Sherpa, they want to receive those messages.

"72 percent of consumers say they *like* to receive promotional messages from brands through email (compared to less than 20 percent from social media)."

Seventy-two percent is a big chunk!

Benefits of email marketing

- Email is one of the least expensive ways to connect with your readers.
- Email enables you to build long-term relationships with your readers.
- Your email list is the foundation of your author platform. It's actually the reason you need a website and blog—to grow your email list.
- Email is hands-down your number one sales tool. (Your blog is your number one marketing tool. Seriously.)
- You own your email list and have full control over it. You do not own your Facebook author page or your Twitter profile or any other social media platform profile.
- Building an email list should be your number one platform-building goal.

How to start your email list

Again, the purpose of this book isn't to teach you how to market, but because platform building is vital to winning the hearts of publishing professionals, I'm going to take a few minutes to give an overview of how to get started with list-building.

- Set up a lead capture system. This is where you will collect the names and email addresses of those who want to join your email newsletter list.
- Use a reputable email delivery service with an autoresponder to deliver a welcome message as soon as someone joins your list. Some of the recommended services include MailChimp, MailerLite, ConvertKit, Aweber, Sendinblue, and others. Each one has different features and pricing. Most offer some sort of free level, or at least a free trial period. Do a bit of research and find one that suits your needs. Many who are new to list-building choose MailerLite or Sendinblue because they allow more features at the free level than other services. But as your list grows (which is the goal), you will eventually have to pay. This is an investment in your career.
- You may also write a series of follow-up messages, spaced a few days apart, that offer the new members a bit more information about you, your writing, and what to expect as far as future content from you. This is called an onboarding sequence.
- You'll need a signup form on your website. Your email service will output a code that you can place in a widget area. If you're unsure how to do all of this, the email service will likely have tutorial videos.
- Create a free giveaway to entice site visitors to join your list. This is called a Lead Magnet. People are wary of giving away their email addresses for no reason. Create a gift that someone will really want. Perhaps a short story that includes characters from one of your books, such as a prequel or maybe develop the story of a secondary character. This free giveaway should look professional and be of high quality—something a reader would be

willing to pay for. There are many available tools you can use, such as Canva, to create it.
- Write your welcome message, and (optional) your onboarding sequence.
- Keep it legal. Email marketing is "permission-based." In other words, you must have permission from people before sending out commercial emails. (And if you're building a list for the ultimate purpose of promoting a book, product, or service, your emails are considered commercial.) This process of granting a list owner permission is called "opting in."

I'd love to share more details with you about list-building and how to use your email list to market books, but because marketing isn't the focus of this book, we need to move that conversation elsewhere.

I've developed a document that explains how to entice readers to join your email list; gives some great lead magnet ideas for authors; shares tips about creating lead magnets and nurturing your list members; what to say in your emails to keep your readers excited about your content; how to structure your emails (a handy template); how often to send emails to your list; and a gameplan of how to make your platform pieces work together—social media, website, blog, and email newsletter list.

The best part of this document is that it's absolutely free! Click this link to get yours now: gatekeepers.link/gameplan. Oh, and yes, you'll need to opt in to our email list to get your free gameplan.

Do you see what I did just then? ;)

Go ahead and click the link. I'll wait right here while you take a minute to sign up and download your free document ...

You're back? Great! Thanks for joining our email list. I hope you find the content useful.

Understand the Basics of Book Marketing

Other important lists to build

In addition to building your newsletter list, there are two more powerful lists authors should work to grow: Amazon and BookBub followers. You won't be able to do that until you have at least one of your titles either published or available for pre-order in an eBook format. As soon as that happens, start encouraging your audience to follow you on these two platforms.

Although Amazon doesn't let authors know how many followers you have, they do send out direct emails to those followers whenever you have a new release. They may also send emails at other times, such as when your Kindle edition is on sale or if you have a book on pre-order.

BookBub, however, shares the number of followers an author has. One of the first goals in building your platform is to get your BookBub followers up to one thousand. Once you've reached the 1000-follower mark, you (or your publisher) can submit a pre-order alert. This is a paid feature of BookBub, but it's cheap. Just a couple of pennies per follower. The first time I used this feature for one of our authors, the number of Kindle pre-orders was four times that of her previous book. (BookBub promotions are for digital titles only at this time.)

BookBub and Amazon both have many powerful promotional features. It's worth the effort to grow those two lists.

There are many aspects to building an author platform, but when I look at the marketing section of a proposal, the first things I want to know are (1) Does the author have a professional-looking website and (2) How many subscribers are on the author's email list?

One last thing before I wrap up this long chapter. Many authors are unsure about what to include when building (or having someone build) an author website. I've made a list of 15 must-haves for author websites that you can download for free by visiting this link: gatekeepers.link/websites

Wrapping it Up

Marketing and selling are not the same thing. Marketing can lead to sales, but it also boosts brand awareness and builds trust in your readers.

- **Takeaway One:** The more people get to know you, the more they will like you. The more they like you, the more likely they are to buy your products.

- **Takeaway Two:** While social media has its place in the author's marketing toolbox, it is not your most powerful tool.

- **Takeaway Three:** Growing and nurturing an effective email list is the best way to increase your book sales.

Chapter 18

Understand the Responsibilities of an Author

Congratulations! You've accepted an offer and signed a publishing contract! You have successfully won the heart of a publisher!

Now what?

Just as the publisher has specific obligations to the author, the author also has responsibilities. Fulfilling those expectations in a timely manner with professionalism and a good attitude will further endear you to your publisher.

Invest in your career

If your goal is to write the one book on your heart, then you should probably self-publish. Publishers are seeking career writers. Those who are willing to invest time, effort, and yes, even money, to improve their craft and promote themselves and their books.

I've met a lot of authors throughout the years who were afraid to spend any money to improve their writing or build their platforms. But remember, anything in life takes time, effort, and oftentimes, money.

Understand the Responsibilities of an Author

I have literally seen people in tears because some free shiny object they signed up for in order to save a few dollars later turned out to be a disaster. Sometimes "free" costs too much.

Become a better writer

Writing is a skill. A craft. And it's a craft that can be improved upon and developed. Many books have been written on the craft of writing. Set a goal of reading at least one such book per month. Do the exercises. Practice.

Another great way to improve your writing skills is to attend classes, conferences, and take online courses. Learn from those with more experience than you. Study at the feet of a bestseller. Take a successful author to lunch, if you can. Subscribe to newsletters and blogs of successful authors in your genre.

One of the most important things aspiring authors can do is read. Read. Read. Read. Don't limit yourself to just the genre you wish to be published in. Read in a variety of genres. Read classics. Read new releases that have hit the bestseller list. Read past bestsellers. Great writers are voracious readers.

Seek feedback. One thing that has baffled me throughout my years in the publishing industry is meeting a would-be author who has never requested feedback from his or her writing. Some think because they made good grades in high school English, they can write a bestseller.

Successful authors are perpetual learners. To become successful yourself, study the craft, learn from the masters, read, and get feedback. You'll be well on your way to growing a great writing career, and you will definitely win the heart of publishers!

Build your platform

What, exactly, is an author platform? As I've mentioned in another part of this section, a platform gives you visibility. This is crucial in a crowded field of authors, with more joining the throng daily.

Basically, an author's platform is a system that works together to build that visibility. Many elements comprise this system: your website, blog, newsletter list, social media platforms, speaking, etc.

Do your research

If you've read this statement a half-dozen times so far during this section, there's a good reason for the repetitiveness. So many writers don't spend the ten-or-less minutes it takes to read the submissions guidelines on a publisher's website. Don't be one of those!

Be easy to work with

Most publishers have some sort of policies and procedures document or guidelines that authors need to comply with. Our P&P document includes information about our staff and their roles; methods of communications (Facebook group, monthly author chats via Zoom, etc.); our editorial and cover design processes; how we do pre-orders; how to purchase author copies; and the list goes on.

Each one of those guidelines has a purpose, a reason it made the list. And those guidelines and processes apply to all our authors.

One of the small publishing house owners I know told me of an author who bucked her at every step in the publishing process, even though the guidelines had been explained during the acquisitions process. This author could not accept the fact that she (a debut author) was to be treated in the same manner as the other authors. My friend went through a lot of grief, at first, trying to please Diva Author, and soon, trying to get rid of her.

The author's rights were reverted almost immediately after her first book with the company was released. Now that author is self-published, which is probably best.

There is nothing wrong with asking questions if you don't

understand something. I welcome questions from our authors and even suggestions on how things can improve. But don't walk in the door with a critical eye and immediately try to change the way your publisher operates. That won't win them over.

Be professional

Professionalism is another way to win the hearts of a publisher. The appearance of your proposal, your website, and even your email address, show your seriousness about your career. If you interact in person or on the phone or via Zoom, let your professionalism shine through.

When you sign with a publisher, both your name and the publishing house's name will be on the book cover. You represent each other. Do your best to represent yourself and your publisher (and agent, and editor) in a professional manner.

Be teachable

If you've ever worked with a know-it-all, you understand how frustrating that can be. No one knows it all. I've been involved with publishing for twenty years, and I learn something every day. Most authors enjoy learning new things, which is good.

But I've run across a few who think they know more about certain things or who question every policy. People with that attitude may find themselves reading a rejection letter, no matter how intriguing their proposal is.

Be a team player

One of the things I love about the publishing industry is the attitude of helping each other. I've seen multi-published authors take time to share tips with an aspiring author. I've drunk coffee with bestselling, award-winning authors, even when I was a newbie to the business. The publishing industry is, in many ways, a big family. A team.

And helping your teammates helps everyone win. Easy ways to help each other include sharing social media posts. Answer questions for new authors. Ask questions of more experienced authors. Read the books of your fellow authors and leave a review. Post encouraging comments to each other's social media profiles. Join launch teams.

We have a small but growing publishing house, and one of the best compliments I get from our authors is that we have a family atmosphere and that nearly everyone is willing to help others. Being a team player will score big points with potential publishers.

Be respectful

Publishers are busy. I understand that most people today are busy, and I've had a lot of busy jobs throughout my life. But I will say that I work more hours owning and operating a small publishing company than I have in any other position I've worked in.

I mentioned earlier that I welcome questions from our authors, and I do. One thing I appreciate about each and every one of them is, nearly every email or text I get starts with, "I know you're busy, so no rush, but …" And then they ask the question. I do my best to respond within at least a day or two. Sooner if I notice the question is time sensitive. But my authors respect my time, and I do my best to respect theirs. Respect goes a long way toward winning someone's heart.

Wrapping it Up

Just as the publisher has specific obligations to the author, the author also has responsibilities. Fulfilling those expectations in a timely manner with professionalism and a good attitude will further endear you to your publisher.

- **Takeaway One:** Publishers are seeking career writers. Those who are willing to invest time, effort, and yes, even money, to improve their craft and promote themselves and their books.

- **Takeaway Two:** Writing is a skill. A craft. And it's a craft that can be improved upon and developed.

- **Takeaway Three:** Your platform gives you visibility so readers can notice you and your books. This is crucial in a crowded field of authors, with more joining the throng daily.

Chapter 19

Understand How to Connect with Publishers

I'm going to let you in on a little secret. One of the little-known facts in the publishing industry is that out of all the gatekeepers standing guard between an author and a published book, the small press owner is probably the easiest to connect with.

The thing is, publishers *want* to see proposals for great books. We really do. Because producing books is how we make money. And, for many small publishers—especially those in niche markets or religious affiliates—books are the best way to promote their message. It's a ministry. So don't be afraid to approach a publisher with a great idea.

Besides, publishers are regular people. Some think I live a glamorous life. I do get to travel a fair bit. And participating as a faculty member at several conferences each year has its perks. But the best part, for me, is sitting across from an aspiring author. The hope. The dream. The passion for her project. It's all wrapped up in a ball of nerves as she digs through her bag, searching for that elusive one sheet, or listening while he muddles through his elevator pitch.

There are several ways to connect with publishers. Some have already been covered in this book—submitting with an agent, getting an editor's attention. But most small publishing companies accept submissions directly from authors.

Unsolicited Submissions

An unsolicited submission is any query or proposal that an editor, agent, or publisher didn't specifically request. Many authors will browse through a market guide and search for the contact information for publishing houses. Some will use an Internet search engine. Others ask fellow authors for publisher recommendations.

Personally, I don't mind unsolicited submissions as long as they fit our guidelines. I recently received an email query from a publicist that began with the words, "Dear Publisher." (Hint: This is NOT the best way to request a publisher to consider your proposal.) The next few paragraphs included some *blah-blah-blah* about the media group's credentials (which I skimmed past) and finally, the message got to the "book" pitch. I put the word book in quotes because, although the publicist used that term, he also said this "quick and easy read" was just 746 words. That's barely three pages!

And some writers wonder why they receive rejections. ***heavy sigh***

Publishers do want to see your proposals, but they don't want you to waste their time. Do your research. Make sure your manuscript fits within their publishing guidelines. Prepare your query in a professional manner. Finally, hit send.

Submissions via Website

Another way to contact many small publishers is through a website submissions form. We have one, and it asks a lot of questions. Why? Because publishers (and the authors who are submitting to us) are busy, getting as much information as possible upfront can save time.

When you do submit, please be patient. If the timeframe stated on the publisher's website has passed, it's perfectly fine to send a follow-up email and ask about the status of your proposal.

Requested Submissions

One of the best ways to connect with a publisher is at conferences, whether in person or at a virtual conference. We have taken many pitches via Zoom at virtual conferences, but now that in-person conferences are returning to normal, publishers can meet authors face to face to discuss their projects.

Again, be sure to check the publisher's guidelines before requesting an appointment. Conference appointment times are limited, so don't waste your chance to meet with an editor, agent, or publisher who is seeking what you're pitching by picking someone who isn't the right fit for your work.

What not to do

It would be comical if things like this never happened, but one big "Don't Do This" when approaching a publisher is pushing your proposal beneath a bathroom stall. While this has never happened to me, I have heard stories from other publishing professionals who were approached in restrooms. Seriously. You'd think it wouldn't be necessary to address such a scenario in this section, but apparently some would-be author thought a conference bathroom break would be a good place to approach a publisher for a one-on-one consultation. That author was wrong.

Wrapping it Up

One of the little-known facts in the publishing industry is that out of all the gatekeepers standing guard between an author and a published book, the small press owner is probably the easiest to connect with.

Understand How to Connect with Publishers

- **Takeaway One:** Most small publishing companies will accept submissions directly from authors.

- **Takeaway Two:** Publishers do want to see your proposals, but they don't want you to waste their time. Do your research. Make sure your manuscript fits within their publishing guidelines.

- **Takeaway Three:** One of the best ways to connect with a publisher is at conferences, whether in person or at a virtual conference.

Chapter 20

Understand How to Beat the Odds

In the first chapter of this section, I shared the odds of getting published traditionally. But there are ways you can significantly increase your odds of landing in that small percentage of authors whose manuscripts are accepted for publication.

Before you attempt to connect with a publisher, the first step is to write a great book. That may sound like a joke, but I'm serious. The book market may *seem* flooded, but it's not flooded with great books. The key is to give your book buoyancy.

If it's been a minute since you took high school physics, buoyancy is the state where an object's "upthrust" is equal to gravity's downward force. The deeper the water, the more pressure increases because the liquid itself is heavy. So, if your book is dense (a nice way of saying "it's terrible"), it'll sink into the mire and never be noticed.

However, if you do what's necessary to overcome the downward forces pushing your book into the depths, you can enable it to rise to the top of the book world floodwaters and float.

So, what can you do to make your book great?

Understand How to Beat the Odds

Hone Your Writing Skills

The first and foremost thing is to study the craft of writing. And it is a craft. Some writers have more aptitude and some natural storytelling talent, but writing can be learned.

Learn what great writing consists of. Proper word usage. Conciseness. Good grammar. Evoking an emotional response from the reader. Learn all the things—and practice.

Get feedback on your writing. Not just from your grandma or your best friend (unless they are bestselling authors). Join a critique group. Pay a multi-published author for a manuscript critique. Enter contests. Hire a freelance editor. It's hard to judge our own work. Painful, even. Sir Arthur Quiller-Couch coined the popular writing advice phrase (often attributed to William Faulkner), "Murder your darlings." *Ouch!*

But honing your craft is the only way to overcome the negative force of bad writing that will drag your manuscript to the depths.

Be Professional

Professionalism is another way to boost your book's buoyancy. A book proposal is akin to a job interview. And every bit of your proposal should embody professionalism from the font to the format. Even your email address should be professional. If a writer's email address is toosexyformyshirt@whatever.com, would you take him seriously?

For more on proposals, refer to the chapter titled, "Understanding How to Connect with Publishers."

Do Your Research

If you wish to get a job as an optometric technician, you wouldn't apply at a dental office. You may think it's ludicrous to even mention such a gaffe, yet every day publishers receive proposals from aspiring authors that are as far from the publishing house's brand as east is from west.

Write a Great Book

I know I mentioned the importance of writing a great book at the beginning of this chapter, but it bears repeating. Because at the end of the day, publishers (and agents, editors, and readers) are lovers of words. So, unless you write a great book, none of the information in this section matters.

Everything in this section has been written with the purpose of helping you learn what it takes to win the heart of a publisher. How to beat the odds. If you write a great story—not a good story, but a great one—you have a much better chance of beating the odds. Great books win the hearts of publishers.

Wrapping it Up

You can significantly increase your odds of getting your manuscript accepted for publication if you follow the advice in this book.

- **Takeaway One:** Before you attempt to connect with a publisher, the first step is to write a great book.

- **Takeaway Two:** Your entire proposal should embody professionalism—from the font to the format.

- **Takeaway Three:** Every day, publishers receive proposals from aspiring authors that are as far from the publishing house's brand as east is from west. Do your research.

Part Three

Winning the Hearts of Editors

By Rowena Kuo

Chapter 21

Introduction to Winning the Hearts of Editors

My older brother holds the claim as my very first client. Five and a half years between us, we arrived in this country with him in first-grade at the age of six, and I had just turned one. Because he understood very little English, he repeated two early grades and struggled throughout school. He did not enjoy reading at all. My parents worked double shifts, and my grandmother, who spoke no English, raised us as my parents worked during those first rough years. My grandmother and I learned English together, watching daytime soap operas and Harry Caray on the Chicago Cubs while my brother battled through school.

Although I hate to admit it, I owe my love for stories to daytime TV. Think about daytime TV for a moment. My grandmother's favorite soap opera started production in 1963, and continues to this day. That means the writers for that show must hold the interest of the audience continually in order for the show to remain on air. So, too, should authors hold that mindset and vision to stand the test of time for their work to become immortal.

I have a theory that memory begins at language acquisition. I learned to read and write at an early age. I love books. I remember the first time my parents took me to a public library, and I thought I had been raptured. I raced up and down the aisles and ran my hand along all the book spines. My family must have thought I'd gone insane. I would say that to be an editor, one has to first love reading. I propose that to be a good writer, one doesn't have to be a good editor, and to be a good editor, one doesn't have to be a good writer. What unifies excellent writing and editing is to be a prolific reader, understanding how words flow together and in what combinations those words have the greatest impact.

When my brother reached high school, he asked me to help him with creative writing, essays, and term papers. He studied hours and hours just to achieve a passing grade. I never knew a more diligent and driven student than my brother. He recognized his weaknesses and used his strengths to overcome those weaknesses. Never one to procrastinate, if he had a paper due at the end of the semester, he would have a rough draft to me the first week. If I had a paper due at the end of the semester, I would wait until the night before the due date and stay up writing, only to have it printed five minutes before class started. I would still get the A, but my weakness centered around procrastination.

I jeopardized my heath and killed countless brain cells just by lack of sleep while my brother fought hard to stay healthy and keep every single brain cell he had because, according to him, he needed every single one to survive. So we struck a deal. I would help him get the A, and he would help me with pacing my homework. This arrangement lasted throughout our high school and college careers. Whenever he received an A for a paper, he would treat me to dinner with his friends. Me, a high school kid hanging out with college kids. I have the best brother in the world.

Only after he graduated college did my brother admit to me that he didn't always get an A. One time, a college professor asked him to stay after class. The professor had compared my brother's in-class writing to the paper he turned in from home and confronted him about plagiarism. My brother confessed that his little sister edited his writing and presented the professor a stack of all his rough drafts with my red-pen edits. Impressed by my brother's hard work, the professor did not expel him and had no problem with my brother having an editor, but she insisted he must cite the editor. Because he didn't cite me from the beginning, a B would be the highest grade my brother would achieve for the paper. My brother had treated me out to dinner with his friends anyway, as if he had received an A.

But what did that teach me? We as editors must be careful not to edit out author's voice. Since then, I have worked for the development of authors and screenwriters to perfect their art. I speak from my own experience in the publishing industry, and although I can't promise you will get published, I hope that if you never give up, there are no barriers to achieving your dreams.

When it comes to editors as gatekeepers to publishing, let's first discuss the various types of editing services and how authors can maximize this knowledge on the road to publication.

Wrapping it Up

What unifies excellent writing and editing is to be a prolific reader, understanding how words flow together and in what combinations those words have the greatest impact.

- **Takeaway One:** Editors must be careful not to edit out author's voice.

- **Takeaway Two:** If you never give up, there are no barriers to achieving your dreams.

Chapter 22

The Acquisitions Editor

Most publishing houses have an acquisitions editor who reviews which manuscripts are good candidates for the house to publish. An acquisitions editor is the main person all submissions go to for consideration in a publishing house. The role of the acquisitions editor is to acquire books that would sell well and enrich the publishing house with quality publications, so, they are, essentially, the publishing house's gatekeeper.

It is critical that you understand the role of this individual in your quest for publication. It is always best to look at the house's guidelines to first see if your manuscript fits what the house is looking for. Review the genres the house publishes and the particular requests the acquisitions editor seeks. Check if the house accepts simultaneous submissions, aligns with your goals for your manuscript, and offers contracts that suit your vision.

Where do you find acquisition editors? The best place would be to attend writers' conferences. You can research editors ahead of time, and, depending on the conference, you can get two or more appointments with writing professionals included in your conference fees. Do your homework. Know what professionals will be at the conference and who would best relate to your book. Research them online and discover who they are to maximize your connection. Find other books the acquisitions editor has acquired and write down the similarities. Explore your genre and see what books align with yours.

Use the Internet to find writers' conferences close to you. They vary in price, accommodations, food, speakers, and length. Research the speakers and the classes. Take advantage of your time at the conference and build those connections. You may have to arrange childcare or get time off from your day job to attend. But the investment in a writers' conference is immeasurable. You develop networks, gain inspiration, meet bestselling authors, hone your craft, and grow your platform.

A word about platform.

A platform is your fanbase of readers who would buy your book and spread word about it to others. It is where you have influence, high regard, and trust from those who follow your work. A platform could be a blog, which is a writer's venue where you express your ideas. It could be a vlog, which is a video version of a blog. It could be your church group, book club, or social media outlets, people who want to know what you have to say and will invest in you to hear more. Some acquisitions editors look at your platform and will use that to gauge what your readership would be. If you don't already have a platform, a writers' conference is a great place to start. Take classes on growing your platform. Sometimes it can take years and multiple books to grow a following.

I have witnessed an author with over 240,000 followers on their platform, but their book did not have many sales. I have also seen an author, who started without a platform at all, grow to become a bestseller. You can succeed or fail, but the consistency of being present for your fanbase is critical for your work to spread.

Are you an introvert or an extrovert?

I have heard that an introvert is a shy person while an extrovert is more outgoing. But I take that a step further. If you are an outgoing person, but you recharge by being alone, then you may be an introvert. If you are a shy person, but you recharge by being in a crowd of people, you may be an extrovert. What makes you an introvert vs an extrovert is how you are recharged. However you recharge, build the relationship with your fanbase. The more you grow your platform, the higher the sales you will potentially have.

Ten percent of published books make back the monetary investment placed into them. So, 90 percent of published books rely upon that 10 percent to keep the publishing house open. The pressure on the acquisitions editor is to find books that sell. The harsh reality of the publishing industry is that many houses rise and fall due to the choices made by their acquisitions editors.

There are so many aspects of writing, and editing is just one. Take classes on editing. If you feel that editing is not your skillset, the better you understand the nuances of editing, the more powerful and effective your writing will be. Take some time to gain a thorough understanding of the editing process. Most writers' conferences will offer a recording of all the classes, so if you miss any classes, you can listen to them later at your own convenience.

Another place to find acquisitions editors is a market guide that lists publishers and their submission processes. These market guides are updated yearly and become an invaluable resource for any author. Every writer should have the *Chicago Manual of Style*, and, for Christian authors, the *Christian Writer's Manual of Style,* as part of their writing library.

What do acquisitions editors look for?

Apart from the specifics of each establishment, I have narrowed down the top three attributes I look for in a fiction manuscript. I'll discuss each one in detail.

1. A believable and satisfying story arc.
2. Deep, well-fleshed-out characters.
3. Author's voice.

Story Arc

I will often see a manuscript with a great start, but then it sags in the middle and ends in a confusing or rushed manner. Pinpoint where your story starts. You are the creator of your characters. You know when they were born and when they die. Show me a segment of that character's life and why I should read about it.

Every story must have conflict. There is no story if there is no conflict. Let's look at the 3-Act Story Arc.

- In Act 1, we answer the following questions: Who is the main character? Give us an introduction as to age, gender, setting, and circumstances. Your character has an everyday life. What does your main character want? What are their dreams and goals that we will journey with them in attaining throughout the story? What is their call to action, and why is that character the only person who can answer this call? And how do we see your character leave on a journey to accept the call? Something interrupts your character's present existence. This is the point where we realize there is no turning back to the life your main character once had. They *must* go forward and embark to a new world, a different set of circumstances. What is obstructing your character from getting what they want?

- In Act 2, what is the first problem they face once they are in their new world? What is their status change, as in how is that opposite of what they were in their old world? List three more problems they will face as they seek to gain the thing they want. What is their moment of maximum angst—that moment they are ready to give up? And what's that glimmer of hope that prompts them to try one last time?

- In Act 3, how does your character achieve or lose the thing they want the most? This is why we must know what they want at the beginning of the story.

Deep, well-fleshed-out characters

Each main character and all supporting characters must have a personality that is distinct from each other. They must have a full range of emotions and their own implied history.

When, in my junior year of high school, I told my parents I wanted to join the publishing industry, they looked at each other and nodded, saying they could see me doing that. However, they said that writing and publication is a fantastic hobby, but I should do something that offers a sustainable paycheck.

So, I went to nursing school and practiced as an RN, BSN for over twenty years. My first job out of nursing school happened to be in a Multiple Personality Psych unit, or Dissociative Disorders. I witnessed, first-hand, patients with more than one person living inside one body. These "alters" would have different handwriting, could be left-handed or right-handed, even changes in eye color and different allergies from the main personality. The ultimate goal in therapy was to integrate all the alters.

I mention this experience because it taught me to discern in a manuscript what characters can stand on their own and which ones can be integrated into one character. If two characters in your story are similar, you may need to eliminate one. Their behaviors should be consistent but not stereotypical. They should have justifiable motives and they should develop as your story progresses.

Author's Voice

What is Voice? Voice is the unique and inherent resonance that the author creates, invoking emotion, empathy, and eagerness within the reader to remain loyal from first word to last in a given work.

Is author's voice a gift or a skill? Are we born with perfect pitch? Can one learn perfect pitch? My older son has perfect pitch. He played the saxophone from grade school through sophomore year in high school. He can listen to a tune once or twice and can either whistle it or play it by memory. When asked to give me an E, he can whistle, hum, or play an E. He could have taken that gift and played professionally, but he quit band by his junior year. He still has perfect pitch, but he did nothing further to develop it. Does one have to have perfect pitch to become a concert pianist?

I believe author's voice is a gift that can be developed. However, I also believe that author's voice can be developed as a skill for those who don't have an inherent gift for it.

As I mentioned before, I believe memory starts at language acquisition. What we can place into words, our minds can process and retain. This is our ability to remember and process communication. This is a gift. As writers, we use words to develop the relationship between the message we want to express and the recipient of that message, the reader. This is a skill. Our personality—this is a gift. Communication of emotions—this is a skill. Passion is a gift. Pacing is a skill.

Having my grandmother with me in my early childhood, I became bilingual. My mother, who has lived in the United States longer than she had lived in her native country, retains a distinct accent when she speaks English. Her earliest memories were that of her village in the Philippines during WWII. She remembers the day the US soldiers rolled their tanks into the village to declare victory and freedom of the villagers from oppression.

A soldier knelt in front of her and offered her a candy bar. That was the first time she had ever seen blue eyes. From that day, she studied hard to achieve her dreams of becoming a nurse and making her way to the United States. She wanted that American Dream, and when the nursing shortage hit the US in the 1960s, she left my brother, then an infant, and father in the Philippines and traveled to America.

This theory of memory at language acquisition can be extrapolated to author's voice. Having worked with international authors whose native language is something other than English, I found that when these authors write in English as a second language, they have a distinct author's voice that differs from a native English speaker. The reverse would hold true for a person whose primary language is English and the secondary language is not. Translated books would have to capture the original author's voice and remain true to that author's intent. Author's voice is unique, like fingerprints. No two voices are the same, and every character in your books should a different voice.

Wrapping it Up

An acquisitions editor is the main person all submissions go to for consideration in a publishing house. The role of the acquisitions editor is to acquire books that would sell well and enrich the publishing house with quality publications, so, they are, essentially, the publishing house's gatekeeper.

- **Takeaway One:** The best way to find editors is to attend writers' conferences.

- **Takeaway Two:** The top three attributes acquisitions editors look for in a manuscript are a believable and satisfying story arc; deep, well-fleshed-out characters; and a fresh author's voice.

Chapter 23

When Can You Stand Your Ground on Edits?

Every house has its standards, and every acquisitions editor has a vision of what books the house desires. If you're not coachable or teachable, you may find it difficult to find a traditional publisher. If you've exhausted your avenues for traditional publishing, you may want to look at your writing and make some changes. Listening to your editor may be the difference between publishing or not publishing your book.

Having said that, if an issue arises where you refuse to accept suggestions for change, then you can always self-publish your book. Self-publication can be a successful means to get your book to your audience; just understand that you have to do all the work (or hire it done) that a traditional house would do for you. Hybrid publishing houses have also grown in popularity, where the author and the house collaborate to publish the work. The author and the house share the financial burden, as well as the royalties.

In 2008, I worked as a nurse but still held the longing to be in the publishing industry. A friend suggested that I look into writers' conferences. I researched and found a writers' conference in my area and submitted to their essay contest. I won a Cecil Murphy scholarship, which included room, board, and the conference classes. I could not contain my excitement, and people commented for the weeks leading to the conference that I glowed.

While at the conference, I sat in the dining hall with a group of would-be authors, joking about opening up our own publishing house. One person at that table called me a year later and said she indeed would start her own publishing house. She asked if I would be one of her acquisitions editors. Of course, I said yes. When I asked why she chose to ask me, she said that during the critique sessions during the conference where she met me, she noticed I had an eye for talent. I could hear author's voice and develop that in a writer. I spent the time after the conference participating in the publication board of a publishing house, where I read manuscripts, offered critiques, and voted on the house's upcoming publications. Little did I know at the time, this experience helped in the decision for me to help my new boss open her publishing house.

That same year, in 2009, a car rear-ended my car, and I endured physical rehab for six weeks. By the time I called to return to work as a nurse, I had been replaced. We brought my youngest daughter, adopted from China, home a year after the car accident, and because of her special needs, I became her full-time nurse.

Born with Spina Bifida, my daughter cannot feel or move anything from the waist down. She had a hole in the middle of her back, and she had been abandoned at birth under a bridge in the middle of winter. I can only imagine that she cried loud enough for someone to find her. The authorities had her air-lifted to a children's hospital in Shanghai, where they performed the necessary surgeries for her to survive. From that point, I worked in the publishing industry and stayed home to raise my kids. I've been a ghostwriter, screenwriter, acquisitions editor, developmental editor, line editor, proofreader, film producer, and financial literacy advocate. I've worn many hats in this industry, and I write this to encourage you in your publication goals. I've helped to develop three publishing houses and now own one myself. Never in my wildest dreams did I ever imagine I would be where I am today.

Something else that you may consider: You may start out wanting to be an author, but there are so many other roles in the publishing industry that might suit you in addition to writing. One of these roles may be as an editor. If that's something you want to do, contact me, and I can get you started. If you love to read, love to get paid to read, have an eye for grammar, and want to help other authors improve their manuscripts, I'm your gal. Despite my many hats, being an acquisitions editor continues to be the one that remains as a gatekeeper to publication.

But I am not alone in my role. I have a publication board to help in the decision-making process. Along with the top three attributes of story arc, characters, and author's voice, I ask each pub board member to vote yes or no to publication, why or why not. Would they buy the book and recommend it to their friends? The task I like the least in the role of acquisitions editor centers around sending rejection letters. I don't like it at all. So with me, it's never a "no," it's a "not yet." I place submissions on a "shelf" where all pub board members can view the manuscripts, much like a shelf in a bookstore.

Manuscripts that receive the majority of positive votes from the pub board receive a contract for traditional publishing. Manuscripts that don't receive positive votes may benefit from our hybrid publishing community within the publishing house.

But what about the manuscripts that nobody looks at? That says something as well. The pub board is a microcosm of how potential readers may react to a particular book. If no one picks a book from the shelf to read, perhaps the book does not stand out enough and requires more work from the author in its title, description, and presentation.

I present at writers' conferences every year. At one conference in particular, I met an author who wanted to be a poet. She showed me

When Can You Stand Your Ground on Edits?

her poetry, and although poetry is not my specialty, I could tell she would require a great deal of help to develop poetry as a skill. No matter how hard I tried to soften my critique, she cried and told me she was devastated. She said she had written two US patents for inventions she had created, but none of that mattered to her as much as her poetry. She showed me her patents, and I had to stand up and walk around, only to sit back down and stare between the patent in my hands and her silent tears. I asked if she realized there are companies out there that would pay $100,000 a year for a technical writer who can formulate patents for them. Technical writing is a skill that doesn't come easy for most people. I went on and on, all excited for her that she could use her writing skills for lucrative gain. She looked at me and said, "But I want to be a poet."

Perhaps she could write patents for companies and get extra income as she developed her poetry skills. I have no idea if she ever took my suggestion to heart. But her expression at the time told me that poetry was her dream, and I had dashed that dream.

Nobody wants to hear their baby is ugly. As authors, we nurture our stories like we would our children. Every word is precious, and we don't want to eliminate any. By showing our work to an editor, we expose our darlings to criticism and attack. It is important to not take anything said about our writing in a personal way. When we become too attached to a particular scene or character or word choice, we may disregard a valuable critique that could improve our writing.

The ability to take criticism and process it, apply it to our work—that is a skill. If an editor gives you feedback, take what you want and disregard the rest. This is your journey. I can give suggestions all day, but you decide your path. No one can do that for you.

Wrapping it Up

The acquisitions editor and the pub board are a microcosm of how potential readers may react to a particular book.

Getting Past the Publishing Gatekeepers

- **Takeaway One:** If you're not coachable or teachable, you may find it difficult to find a traditional publisher.

- **Takeaway Two:** You may start out wanting to be an author, but there are so many other roles in the publishing industry that might suit you in addition to writing.

Chapter 24

The Developmental or Content Editor

At writers' conferences, I expect to see rough drafts, as that is a big part of the experience. Authors go to conferences to learn and receive help with their manuscripts. However, before you submit your work to an agent or a publishing house, I recommend that you get your manuscript edited and polished. A freelance developmental or content editor can help with that process. They point out loopholes in your story, may suggest rearrangement of chapters, or strengthening of your plot, conflict, and characters.

Where do you find freelance editors? We come in all genres and all budgets. You can find us on social media, through referrals from other writers, and you can find us at writers conferences. A developmental edit can cost you between $300-$2500, depending on word count and the time it would take to edit your book. If writing your novel takes you a year or more, having it edited could take just as long. Be patient. Before you obtain the help of a content editor, a way to improve your manuscript would be for you, the author, to become a Master of Firsts.

Firsts

How many numbers are there between 0 and 1? As there is an infinite number between 0 and 1, so, too, are there infinite word combinations to consider before you even write your first sentence. A Master of Firsts recognizes the gift of infinity to lift the limits off how the story comes to life. What separates failure and greatness falls to just one word: and.

What is your *and*? With what content will you fill your pages? There is infinity between failure and greatness. "And" equals infinity. Decide now that failure is not an option.

You have only one chance to make a first impression, so the opening lines of your work need to have impact. The first sentence intrigues the reader, must be compelling enough to hold the reader's attention, and may or may not be its own paragraph. The first sentence introduces the author's voice. The first line, which sets the tone, can be a quote from a character, and may be in the middle of an action. A Master of Firsts draws the reader in by the first paragraph. Every word matters, so don't waste any. Use strong, active verbs.

An ideal first page has between 100-300 words. You are developing a relationship with your reader. With your words, you are painting a picture of what your characters are experiencing. This establishes a dialogue between you and your reader. Your first page should also establish your Point of View (POV) character.

POV

POV should be one character, one viewpoint, per scene.

In First Person, you write your experiences in a way that you, as your POV character, can instill a sense of empathy for your character in your reader. We, as your reader, become the "I" and "me" in your story. We identify with your first-person character.

In Second Person, you develop a relationship with your reader as if you are in dialogue with your reader. This can be implemented in nonfiction, as I am addressing you, the reader, as I write this. It can also be used in fiction as if writing in a diary or journal. Your reader can empathize with you but is separate from you.

In Third Person, you are the narrator, but your POV character becomes the one the reader identifies with. You may change your POV character at a scene change or at the beginning of a new chapter, but you should avoid head hopping—moving from one character's point of view to another's within the same scene. All feelings and experiences are described from a single POV. What you've established in your first paragraphs should remain consistent whether it is in first, second, or third person.

Even if you are the omniscient narrator, where the author writes from an "all-knowing" perspective, by the end of the first page, zone in on one head. Head hopping distracts your reader, interrupts the relationship your reader is forming with your POV character, and takes your reader out of the world you have created.

- **Here is an example of head hopping:**

> He imagined her traveling the world, meeting intriguing people ... eating exotic food. He wanted a life like that. She hated to travel. She would rather stay home, curl up in her favorite chair, and read a good book.

Note that in the same paragraph, we are in two different heads. Here is an example of how to fix head hopping.

> He imagined her traveling the world, meeting intriguing people ... eating exotic food. He wanted a life like that.
>
> "I hate to travel," she said, surprising him. "I'd rather stay home, curl up in my favorite chair, and read a good book."

We stay in one head throughout the scene. A Master of Firsts

The Developmental or Content Editor

captures the reader, sets up the conflict in the story, and establishes POV in the first chapter. In essence, a Master of Firsts is a Master of POV.

I propose that the difference between the novelist and the screenwriter is Point of View. The novelist writes from the inside, looking out. The screenwriter writes from the outside, looking in. The novelist has a natural command of POV due to the introspective nature of the POV character. The screenwriter sees all, knows all, and writes as if directing actors on a stage what to do and where to go.

If you have issues with POV, then you may be a natural screenwriter. When I read a submission, I can often tell if a novelist has a screenwriter's eye. I encourage any novelist with an issue maintaining POV to try screenwriting. The world needs screenwriters too. Check out screenplays from your local library to get a sense of structure and format and see if your manuscript adapts better for the screen. The publication avenue may be different, but films are a form of publication, nonetheless.

But I digress.

A Master of Firsts follows a mini story arc in the first chapter, which has a beginning, middle, and end, with a cliffhanger that leads to the next chapter.

A content editor will help you determine where your story should begin. Some houses suggest an author remove the prologue. In deciding whether or not to remove the prologue, ask yourself, "Does it move the story forward? Can I integrate the prologue into the main story?"

An effective way of using a prologue is what I call the Apex Hook. The Apex Hook is taking the pinnacle point of the story and turning that into the prologue. Then, in your first chapter, going back to a point before that event and leading your reader toward the Apex Hook.

Every chapter should have a cliffhanger ending which will compel your reader to the next chapter. Your reader wants to know, "What will happen in the next chapter?"

Chapter one doesn't have to be very long. A first chapter could be between 300-5000 words. A Master of Firsts applies this formula to every chapter: A strong first line with a beginning, middle, and ending with a cliffhanger, which the author implements throughout the book.

If you are a Master of Firsts, you will also be a Master of Lasts. A good ending should satisfy the reader as a stand-alone book, even if it is part of a series. The ending should tie all loose ends together and give the reader closure. It should make your reader want to read the story again or await the sequel. If your goal is publication, become a Master of Firsts.

A good content editor will also suggest avoiding "ly" adverbs. These tend to "tell" when you want to "show." A good exercise would be to highlight every "ly" adverb and see if you can change each instance to avoid them. Common ones are "suddenly, quickly, quietly." If you must use an "ly" adverb, use one that is uncommon, and use it once per manuscript.

Another issue a content editor might point out is how to avoid backstory. Backstory consists of the circumstances, events, and consequences that lead up to the main story. Backstory interrupts your main story and pulls them out of your book. It slows down the pace when you want to keep the reader's interest. What to do if you have backstory? Delete it. Go through the manuscript and take it out. Think of it as de-weeding. Backstory can choke your main story just like weeds can choke a garden.

Ways to Recognize Backstory

The Flashback: A flashback is the sudden shift to past events. If you must use a flashback, make it just that, a flash. Nothing more than one sentence. And it should be in relation to a current action that moves the main story.

- **Here is an example of Backstory in Flashback:**

Mike hesitated but then sprinted after Joe to the backyard. Joe grabbed onto the lowest branch of the towering oak and swung a leg over it. Suddenly, Mike was eight years old all over again, and he fell out of the neighbor's tree. It had rained the night before, and the branches had been slick. He wore a cast for six weeks after that. He wasn't sure he would ever get over it. Aunt Myrtle visited him and brought her homemade chocolate chip cookies. He liked chocolate chip cookies ...

In this example, we have lost connection to the main story, and the author has taken the reader down a detour. A flashback gives the reader an opportunity to put the book down, and they may or may not return.

Another way to recognize backstory is called the Dream Sequence. A dream sequence usually begins a chapter. It seems real before the character comes to some realization and awakens. It is considered cliché, so avoid this method as much as possible.

A third way backstory may sneak into your manuscript is what I call the Aside. An aside interrupts your main story to relay events and circumstances leading to the scene. This is an information dump to your reader to catch them up to the story, so this is an example of "telling" when you want to "show." An aside may be transitioned by the words, "S(he) or I remembered when ..." As authors, we must restrain the urge to explain.

- **Here is an example of an Aside:**

Mike hesitated but then sprinted after Joe to the backyard. Joe grabbed onto the lowest branch of the towering oak and swung a leg over it. Mike remembered when he was eight years old, and he fell out of the neighbor's tree. It had rained the night before, and the branches had been slick. He was in a cast for six weeks after that. He wasn't sure he would ever get over it.

If backstory must be included in the manuscript, there are effective ways to incorporate past events.

- **Begin earlier.** Decide where the heart of your story begins and start there. Write chronologically, and don't look back.

Here is a fix to backstory using the technique of starting the story earlier:

Eight-year-old Mike fell out of the neighbor's tree, its branches slick from the rain the night before. He wore a cast for six weeks after that. He wasn't sure he would ever get over it. Years later, Mike hesitated, but then sprinted after Joe to the backyard. Joe grabbed onto the lowest branch of the towering oak and swung a leg over it.

- **Dialogue and action.** The best way to incorporate a short backstory is through dialogue and action. Use an existing scene to bring out the past through the dialogue and actions of the characters.

Here is an example of fixing backstory through dialogue and action:

Mike hesitated but then sprinted after Joe to the backyard.

"We were eight when you fell out of the neighbor's tree," Joe said as he grabbed onto the lowest branch of the towering oak and swung a leg over it. "Not a bit slick today."

"I was in a cast for six weeks," Mike said, refusing to look past that first branch. "I don't think I'll ever get over it."

- **Apex Hook.** As mentioned, the Apex Hook is taking a section from the middle of the book, usually the culminating action point, using a portion of this as the prologue, and then the backstory becomes the main story leading to that apex moment. Be careful that the main story leading up to the apex moment is just as intriguing as your apex hook. Upon reaching the apex of the story, you finish what you left hanging in the apex hook and resolve the rest of the story.
- **Simultaneous Storylines.** This is the best way to incorporate large sections of backstory. Break the past and the present by alternating or placing periodic chapters. Make the time period clear. This method can be very confusing to the reader, but if done well, can be an effective tool to integrate backstory. In alternating chapters, you could have dual protagonists and dual time periods. You could also have one protagonist and dual time periods. The past story must intertwine with the present story in a relevant way. To incorporate a moderate amount of backstory, you can use periodic chapters to reflect the past every third or fourth chapter. These, too, must intertwine with the present story.
- **Character as Narrator.** In this method, one of the characters narrates a story from the past, and for a brief moment, tells a story within the main story. The other characters listen in rapt attention. This shouldn't be more than a few pages of text, and it must be relevant to the main story.

Dialogue

Another issue a content editor helps with is dialogue. Dialogue is the verbal exchange between the characters of a given work, taking into consideration vernacular, societal influence, and idiosyncrasy that is both believable and compelling. Dialogue establishes the relationship between your characters in relation to your POV character, given the nature of the setting. Dialogue should have a purpose and a chemistry of interaction.

The stages of relationship are as follows:

1. **First impressions:** Attraction. Your characters are drawn together for a common purpose or goal.
2. **Relationship:** Harmonization. Your characters fight together and align themselves against a common enemy.
3. **Conflict:** Dissonance. The characters face some disagreement, a point in the story where a decision is made to go different paths. Your POV or main character is left alone to face the enemy at an unfair disadvantage because of some fault or betrayal.
4. **Story conclusion:** Resolution. The characters come together again to face the common enemy. Trust is restored, and the main character is victorious in achieving his or her goal. Or not. It depends on your view of how the story is resolved. No matter if it ends well or not, the story must have a satisfying ending, and dialogue is key to achieving that end. The chemistry of interaction is to choose your characters, establish relationships, stage those relationships, and find resolution.

Good dialogue should be no more than four lines per character before another one speaks. Each sentence should be able to fit into one breath. Read your dialogue out loud to check. Limit the number of exclamation points. Avoid clichés, awkward phrasing, non-sequiturs, and jarring transitions. Dialogue should flow between one character and the next in a way that makes sense given the region where the story takes place, the time period, the gender of the characters, and their idiosyncrasies.

There is an art to conversation. Be mindful of entertainment value, sentence structure, volume, and timbre. No matter the genre, an element of romance in the storyline adds to reader interest. Having romantic tension in dialogue becomes a key component in building relationships between your characters and your reader.

Romance is one of the most popular genres, and any book you write may do well to have a romantic element in some form within your plot.

Pacing

Content editors will also guide you on the pacing of your story. As your story progresses, varying the action and dialogue keeps the interest of your readers. If the action overwhelms the reader, there may be a desensitization as a result of too much happening without pause. The same goes for lulls or long narratives with nothing happening in the story to hold the reader's attention. Balancing action and introspection of your protagonist is key to the development of your plot.

Build micro-tension into each scene so that your reader feels something big is coming, then deliver it. Each scene of dialogue may be 1-3 pages long before moving the story to a different scene. This holds your reader's attention without overwhelming them. Dialogue is best when held between 2-4 characters at a time. Any more than that per scene can be confusing to a reader trying to remember everybody in your book. Dialogue should serve one or two purposes, including entertainment, character development, relationship development, information, introspection, intent, and expression.

Research

Developmental editors may point out areas where more research might benefit your story. Research your setting and time period. If the place is fantastical and is a creation of your mind, then formulate physics and rules that are believable. Whether it be theoretical science or superpowers, the set of physics you establish for your world should be based on reality, something any reader would find relatable. When you create your character bios, research various personality traits and experiences that would support their motives

The Developmental or Content Editor

and behaviors. Start from writing about what you know and expand your knowledge base from there.

As an example, I met a 60-year-old male author whose protagonist embodied a 16-year-old girl. She drove a Lamborghini and smoked Cuban cigars. I pointed out that her mannerisms and vernacular reflected that of a 60-year-old man rather than that of a 16-year-old girl. This shows how important it is to write from what you know and research what you don't know.

Avoid Epic Fails

Your content editor may also help prevent issues that can crash your manuscript.

1. **Version Confusion.** We may not notice in our first draft, but our supporting character, Bob, dies in chapter one. Yet in our ninth draft, he reappears in chapter two to save the dog from the house fire. This happens because we have several versions of our manuscript with minor tweaks and forget which version is the most up-to-date. If you save a version where you may use part of it in the final draft, remember to develop a system where you know that version is not the master copy. As I save these versions, I date them and make sure I restart from the most recent version. You may have other ways to note versions, but an issue like this can become difficult to fix, especially once the book comes out in print.
2. **Abrupt Transitions.** These are instances that can give your reader whiplash. Sometimes we don't see these jarring events as everything flows from our heads in a seamless manner, however, we can lose a reader if we don't see things through their eyes. If you have your main character as a clumsy bookkeeper in one scene and an

experienced swordsman in the next, you have not developed that transition in the eyes of your reader.
3. **Lag and Lull.** Avoid long, drawn-out scenes where nothing much happens to move the story forward. If your reader skips the middle to get to the end, then you have lag and lull as a problem in your manuscript.

Passive vs Active Verbs

A content editor will also show you areas where you tend to use passive verbs rather than active ones. An exercise would be to go through your manuscript and highlight every "was," "were," "felt," "seemed," and all forms of "know." All of these are examples of passive verbs. Replace these instances with an action using a strong, active verb.

- **Here is an example of a passive sentence:**

She was intrigued by him.

- **To make this sentence active:**

He intrigued her.

- **Another example of passive:**

He seemed to like her jokes.

- **Make it active:**

He laughed at her every joke.

- **Passive:**

He was running after her.

- **Better:**

He ran after her.

- **Even better:**

He bolted after her.

In each instance, we have improved the sentence from passive to active.

Wrapping it Up

Become a Master of Firsts. Openings are what hook the reader. Your first page, first paragraph, first sentence, first word are vital. Master those firsts.

- **Takeaway One:** Before you submit your work to an agent or a publishing house your manuscript must be edited and polished.

- **Takeaway Two:** A developmental editor points out loopholes in your story, may suggest rearrangement of chapters, or strengthening of your plot, conflict, and characters.

Chapter 25

The Line or Copy Editor

Hair conditioner vs air conditioner: One letter can make a difference. Relying on your writing program's spell-checker may not always work. You need a real person to check your manuscript for errors where the spelling may be correct, but the context isn't. Although you may want to do this all yourself, self-editing is like self-surgery. Not only is it painful, the perspective is all wrong.

The next editor you might want to enlist for your work would be one who specializes in line or copy editing. This editor has an eye for grammar, sentence structure, spelling, and format. Sometimes, when we've read our manuscript over and over again, it's easy to miss something we thought we had already fixed. New eyes can spot these anomalies when our perceptions have already filtered out our errors. Even editors need editors.

Formatting

A line editor will see to it that you have proper formatting. You don't want to be rejected by a publishing house because of a technicality that could have been fixed by a line editor. The standard format for manuscripts includes 1-inch margins, 12-pt Times or Times New Roman font, double-spaced, without extra spaces in between paragraphs. I suggest that you don't use flowery fonts, fancy backgrounds, or emojis in your manuscripts. These tend to distract the eye when the focus should be the story.

Professional Presentation

A copy editor can also review your professional presentation materials.

- **Query Letter.** Here is a standard template for a query letter.

    1. **To:** Editor's or Agent's name, place of establishment, and date
    2. **Contact information:** name, address, phone, email
    3. **Four paragraphs—Paragraph one:** hook, goal, motivation, conflict, theme, introduction of your main characters, what will catch the reader's attention.
    4. **Paragraph two:** Book title, subtitle, tagline, and then a statement about why the establishment would need your manuscript.
    5. **Paragraph three:** Your credentials, why it's you who should write this book.
    6. **Paragraph four:** Ask permission to send your proposal and thank them for considering your submission.
    7. **Finish with your contact information:** Your legal name, your pen name if different than your legal name, address, phone, and email address.

- **Professional One Sheet**

You can use your creative talents on your professional one sheet. Here, you can use your flowery fonts, fancy backgrounds, and artistic elements that you might not use in your manuscripts. A One Sheet is to be printed and given out at conferences, conventions, or places where you would want your manuscript to be acquired by publishing professionals. The way you lay it out is up to you, but here are the elements your one sheet should include:

1. **100-word bio.** Introduce who you are, what you've written, what you do outside of writing, any hobbies, and one line about your life.
2. **Professional headshot photo.** This should be in high resolution. A high-resolution photo will make a clear thumbnail picture or larger, but a low-resolution photo might turn out blurry when the size is needed for more than a thumbnail.
3. **200-word blurb of your story.** This would be a version of your back cover copy or the description of your book on Amazon. This is not a synopsis. This is meant to intrigue readers to buy your book.
4. **Your contact information.** Use your pen name, address, email, and phone. Whatever name you choose will become part of your brand.
5. **Attach a business card.** Include an image of your book cover or some other memorable way can associate you with what you write.

- **Book Proposals**

Your line editor could also check your book proposals. I receive many questions from authors about book proposals. Often, when pub board members have a stack of submissions to wade through, they may not have time to read your book. They first look at your book proposal before deciding to move on to the next submission or continue reading. I ask my pub board readers to read until they don't care to read any further. If at any point they stop reading, that would indicate to the author where to work on revising the story.

What should authors include in a book proposal? Here is a list:

1. **Cover page:** Your cover page should have your title, subtitle, contact information, and, if applicable, agent information
2. **Proposed table of contents:** This is not needed if you haven't named your chapters.
3. **Short synopsis:** This would be equivalent to a 3-minute elevator pitch. Between 300-500 words. Your short synopsis might be the back cover copy of your future book or the description of your book on its Amazon landing page. Your short synopsis answers who, what, where, when, and why, with the content of your book answering how.
4. **Longer synopsis:** This is a chapter-by-chapter summary of your book from beginning to end and should be about a page in length for every 4000 words of text.
5. **About the author:** This includes your education, experience, and any conferences you've attended. This is between 300-500 words and also includes special interests or hobbies, what other work you do besides writing, and a line about your family. Although the last line may be optional, this gives a glimpse of your personality. Sometimes it's not just the contents of a book, it's the author's life, personality, and willingness to build a fanbase that makes a book successful.
6. **Marketing potential:** Who is your intended audience? What age group are you targeting? Think of

your favorite books in your genre. What do they have that makes you want to read them over and over again and tell your friends? Now think of today's bestsellers. What do they have that makes them so popular? One can argue that today's bestsellers are your book's competition. But I argue, what do book lovers want? More books! Let's change our perspective. What if we don't think of it as a competition? More than one million books are published in the US each year. The goal is to align our books with the bestsellers, so the model is more collaborative than competitive. Even if your book publishes traditionally, you will be expected to market your book.

7. **Future book synopsis:** any planned sequels or other books you have written. I encourage authors not to close any doors to sequels even if they intend their book to stand alone. This means don't kill off your main character or create a situation where you cut off any hopes of a sequel. If you never write a sequel, that's fine, but you should not limit yourself or your characters when it comes to more adventures. Leave the future open. Just in case. You never know if the popularity of your book demands a sequel. The goal of sequels is to be better than the book preceding it. If you write a great first book, you have the potential to write an even better second book.

8. **Marketing ideas:** Your platform, church groups, book clubs, critique groups, bookstores, table events, interviews, podcasts, book signings, anything where you could participate in marketing your book.

9. **Character synopsis:** Key players (must have a problem or conflict to resolve). Any supporting characters, such as a sidekick, mentor, or love interest.

10. **Title page:** Of your book. Just the title, subtitle, and your pen name.

The Line or Copy Editor

11. **Sample chapters:** Some publishers and agents will ask for the first 3 chapters. These should be polished and in the best shape possible as these might be the only thing the establishment will look at. If they like it, they will ask for the entire manuscript.
12. **Entire Manuscript:** Some places will ask for the entire manuscript upon submission. Although a fantastic opportunity, your manuscript must be in the best shape possible. From Content to Line Editor, you may also want to include a proofer, or a proofreader.

Proofreader

This is the last type of editor authors turn to before submitting your book to an agent, acquisitions editor, or a publisher. A proofer offers that added protection to help ensure your manuscript has achieved its maximum potential. A proofer will not comment on content or development. Their job is simply to make sure your manuscript has few-to-no errors.

Wrapping it Up

A line editor will check your manuscript for errors where the spelling may be correct, but the context isn't. Although some authors try to do this step themselves, remember—self-editing is like self-surgery. Not only is it painful, the perspective is all wrong.

- **Takeaway One:** While the content/development edit covers the big picture, a line edit zones in on the manuscript line by line. Line editors have an eye for proper grammar, sentence structure, spelling, and formatting.

- **Takeaway Two:** In addition to revising your manuscript, a line editor can help authors prepare their query letter, one sheet, and proposal, and ensure that each is presented professionally.

Chapter 26

Conclusion

When my youngest daughter arrived in the USA at the age of 22 months, she spoke 4 languages: Mandarin, Spanish, English, and Sign. I did not know sign language, but I noticed she moved her hands in a way to indicate something she wanted. In her history, she had been placed into an orphanage after her surgery where she lay for hours daily in her crib without moving. She didn't cry, didn't move, didn't show any facial expression at all. The nannies at the orphanage said that if this baby didn't find a family soon, she would die.

An expat family from Spain applied to be a foster family, and the orphanage sent her to be with that family until she could find a forever family. Being expats, the family could not adopt her under Chinese law. But they could foster her. They reported that when she first came to live with them, she would stare off into space, not looking at anyone or anything in particular. But they poured love on her and spoke to her and cared for her. After the first week, they noticed she began following them with her eyes. She would look at them, so they engaged her even further. In a month, she giggled, played with toys, and began to belly crawl around the house. They

Conclusion

taught her Mandarin, Spanish, and English. She also went on play dates where she picked up words in sign. My daughter still maintains contact with that family, as they are her godparents. Although they have returned to Spain, the Internet keeps contact possible.

When my daughter started physical therapy, her PT said to use her strengths to strengthen her weaknesses. Although she can't move her legs, she has a strong upper body and a sharp mind. She can haul herself up a set of stairs, using her arms, her chin, and her core. She can also win any argument with her older siblings, who are five to ten years older.

I use this as an example where intention and hard work will overcome any adversity. As with publication, writers must be willing to work hard and stay focused on their goals. Are you a better speaker than a writer? Then speak into a recording device and write it down. There are programs that employ voice to script technology. Are you a better writer than speaker? Then whenever you have to talk about your book, write it down and practice your speech.

Sometimes we may not like what an editor has to say to us. If anything I have said has value for you, then great. Any critiques you receive on your writing from editors are just opinions. It is up to you whether or not you will decide what's best for your work.

While waiting for feedback from an editor, continue with your development as an author. Attend writers' conferences, critique groups, and avenues to improve your skills. When searching for a critique group, look for honest feedback. Friends and family may think they're supporting you by giving you only positive feedback, but iron sharpens iron. They may want you to feel good, but would you rather feel good or get your work published? If we're not growing, we're dying. Growth can be painful. And growth continues after your manuscript has been accepted for publication.

Understand that once you have passed the gatekeepers to publishing and have signed a contract, the entire editing process may continue, depending on the publishing house. This means the house may assign an editor to you to go through the manuscript and adapt it to their standards. The difference is that if you have a traditional house, the house pays for the editing. Prior to contract, or with self-publishing or hybrid publishing, you pay for editing. The less the house has to do in order for your book to publish, the sooner you will be published. The less work the house has to invest in your work, the likelier it is to be accepted. From contract to publication can take a year or more. The editing phase alone could be three-fourths of that time. Anything and everything you can do beforehand to cut that time down may help to publish your book sooner.

Of all these tips to improve your writing, the greatest tool to have is your author's voice. I have found bestselling authors, who have broken every writing "rule," amass a huge fan base because of author's voice. They use backstory, have POV shifts, throw "ly" adverbs prolifically throughout their novels, and yet remain on the *NY Times* Bestseller list for weeks after their books hit print. They have a unique author's voice. They grab their readers, and they don't let go. But remember, author's voice is not the goal. It is a side effect. It is a side effect of developing that relationship between your characters and your readers.

What will be your writing legacy?

How will your readers remember you? How do you stand out among all those authors and pull your readers into your world? You cultivate your art. You allow your readers to see you through the lens of what you write.

A new passion of mine is author legacy. If our manuscripts are like our babies, we should plan for them like we would plan for our children. I met an author to whom I sent a contract, but I never heard a response back from her. After several weeks, I found out through social media that she had passed away.

After a time, I tried to contact her family, but no one had any idea she was an author, did not know where she had placed her manuscripts, and knew nothing about nor had any interest in writing.

Conclusion

Imagine if Jane Austen or JRR Tolkien or Ernest Hemingway had passed away without writing their work down on paper. We would not have those classics to read today. I wonder how many great works are trapped in attics and hard drives and shoe boxes all over the world. Or worse, died unwritten.

Authors, don't hesitate to save your life's work in a way that somebody could enjoy them later. Set up a plan for them and provide for them in your wills and trusts and estate plans. Appoint a guardian or an agent to act on your behalf should anything ever happen to you and you can't make decisions for your manuscripts. If you want help to do this, please contact me, and I will help you set that up.

Editors as gate*keepers* to publication can also be the gate*ways* to publication. My job as an editor is to make you, the author, look good. Enlist the right editors to help your writing. Perseverance is sustaining throughout. A steady progression despite adversity. It is unfailing and resistant to pressure. No matter how disheartening achieving publication can be, keep going. The hardest part is persistence. To write is to captivate the soundless through the power of imagination by your personal timeline within your budget, using only words. You've already written the book. You are already an author. Now, go forth through the gate and publish it.

Wrapping it Up

Editors as gate*keepers* to publication can also be the gate*ways* to publication. An editor's job is to make you, the author, look good.

- **Takeaway One:** Intention and hard work will overcome any adversity. Writers must be willing to work hard and stay focused on their goals.

- **Takeaway Two:** No matter how disheartening achieving publication can be, keep going. The hardest part is persistence.

Part Four

Winning the Hearts of Readers

By Carrie Schmidt

Chapter 27

Introduction to Winning the Hearts of Readers

"*M*any people, myself among them, feel better at the mere sight of a book." Like the quoted novelist Jane Smiley, I feel a bit lost without a book nearby. I was blessed with parents and other loved ones who read multiple books to me daily. In fact, one of my first five words was *book*. This delightful saturation of words and pictures, of stories and imagination, has been my life since I was a toddler. Not too many days have gone by that I don't have at least one book on my person. I even ran an unofficial (and probably unsanctioned) fiction-lending library out of my dorm room in college.

Since 2015, when I started ReadingIsMySuperPower.org, I have also been an active part of the book community. In addition to being an avid reader, I am a blogger, a reviewer, a first reader, an influencer, a contest judge, a speaker, a conference coordinator, and a publicity tour company founder. In a nutshell, I get to live, breathe, and sleep books. (Is there any better pastime??) With all the various hats I wear in this industry, I have the privilege of chatting with many authors at different stages of publishing and marketing. No matter the hat or the stage, the question that comes up most frequently in our conversations is, "What can I do to get my book in front of new readers?"

Likely, you've asked this question in your own writing journey, or perhaps you've asked one of these other variations of the same tune:

- How do I find readers who want to read my genre?
- What do I do with readers once I've found them?
- How do I *keep* readers?
- How do I get them to read my book?
- How do I get readers to *buy* my book without selling my soul in the process?
- What draws readers to certain authors, and what turns them away from others?

In our time here together, studying the reader and reviewer gatekeepers of the publishing industry, I hope to equip you with some practical tools that answer those questions. It is also my prayer that you close these chapters with a new appreciation for reviewers, bloggers and Bookstagrammers, and for every reader who invests in a book and can't quit talking about it. After all, to quote author Amanda Dykes, what a reader takes from and brings to a book "makes the story come alive in a magical way that nothing else can even come close to replicating ... Without them, the story equation is incomplete."

On Finding Readers

Before you can get your book in front of new readers, you obviously must *find* them and then plant yourself where they spend time.

Most readers are, by nature, introverted. This is certainly not true for all, but many of us recharge by being alone and, well, reading. We tend to prefer low-contact socializing, but we love to talk about books. We are on most social platforms, and we gravitate toward others who read the same books that we love. While more difficult to find us in person, it's not impossible. We do still love spending hours in libraries, bookstores, and even book festivals. Readers have established active discussion groups on Facebook, creative networks on Instagram and TikTok, and popular hashtags on Twitter. We've also infiltrated the less obvious places you'd look for readers, including a community of over 2 million members who ask others to 'suggest me a book' on Reddit. Readers are everywhere, waiting to be found by you and your books.

In equal turn, however, this 'everywhere-ness' can be overwhelming for authors who already have limited bandwidth. Juggling family life, an additional career or two, writing books, and marketing books doesn't leave much margin, does it? From Facebook to Instagram to TikTok to local festivals and everything in between, how can you best focus your time and energy in looking for readers?

Prioritize

The truth is this: You must filter out some of the options and pick the focus that works best for you. If you don't, you run the considerable risk of burning out on the social/promotion tasks and losing your passion to write those yummy words readers crave. When you do give yourself the freedom to zero in on one or two options, you will invest the largest portion of your budgeted engagement time in platforms that best fit you and your books.

Trying to spend time promoting your work in all the places becomes more like a game of Whac-A-Mole instead of a good return on your time and energy. I understand the fear of missing out on readers through other platforms, but sometimes we are most effective when we become more selective. One of my favorite movie lines of all time (from the 1995 version of *Sabrina*, with Harrison Ford and Julia Ormond) says the same thing a different way: "More isn't always better, Linus. Sometimes it's just more." This is not only true of material things or money; it's also true of book promotion.

Introduction to Winning the Hearts of Readers

Are you most comfortable and most familiar with Facebook? Do you love taking (or looking at) pretty pictures of books on Instagram? Have you dared to brave Twitter and found it valuable for your writing or other areas of your life? Does TikTok feed your creativity? Are you more likely to be on Reddit than Goodreads? Find your sweet spot on social media—that intersection of where you are most comfortable and where the readers of your genre most congregate—and give yourself the freedom to make *that* your target for finding new readers. Feel free to engage on more than one platform if you have the time and energy; just be careful not to spread yourself too thin. And if you reach a point where you feel you've exhausted the benefits of a certain platform or you're ready to stretch your skills elsewhere, it's okay to change your focus.

These principles apply to in-person engagement as well as social media. If you have a great local library system or bookstore, utilize their established outreach resources and schedule a talk or a signing. If you'd rather attend a festival, book related or not, set up a booth to sell your books if it's cost effective to do so. The point is, you shouldn't try to do it all. Prioritize for best results.

It's worth noting here that you still may feel caught in that Whac-A-Mole game as you prioritize through trial and error. However, once you've found the sweet spot we discussed, it should become more of an enjoyable carousel ride. (I call dibs on the purple pony!)

Teamwork

It's also not a requirement to do any of this 'reader seeking' on your own. Team up with your fellow authors for a Facebook party or an Instagram cross-promotion. Share the cost of a festival booth with other local authors. Utilize a paid service like Booksweeps or Author XP and their multi-author giveaway promotions that increase your audience through newsletter subscribers and BookBub followers. (Note: These paid services tend to attract freebie-seekers who will unsubscribe when they don't win. It can still be a good way to get your email list or BookBub numbers started, though, and you will likely retain some of those new subscribers after all.) Writing may be a solitary pursuit, but finding new readers doesn't always have to be.

Another great way to benefit from teamwork and put your work in front of new readers is to do what you do best—write. Collaborate with other authors who write in your genre and release a collection of novellas around a certain theme. (Christmas is a great time for this, by the way. Readers eat up Christmas novella collections like candy.) Ideally, at least one of these contributors should be an anchor author who has a larger audience, but this doesn't have to be the case.

This principle most clearly plays out in the television industry. Networks often sandwich (or 'hammock') a new show between two of their most popular ones in that evening's programming. They are working on the assumption that viewers won't want to change channels, thereby giving the new show a ready-made audience. If those viewers like that first episode sandwiched between their favorite shows, they are likely to stay on as fans. So, too, can a collection of authors gain new readers for each other.

I may have grabbed the book because my favorite author is in it, but I'll read these other three or four stories because I'm already here. Chances are I'll love some of their voices, too, and start hunting for those new-to-me authors' backlists and future releases as a result.

I Found Some Readers. Now What?

I realize that at this point, other than giving you the freedom to prioritize certain avenues of promotion over others, I've likely not yet told you much that you didn't already know. Rest assured that in the remaining chapters of this section, we will be taking an in-depth look at reader engagement (including ideas for social media) and giving you practical ways to win the hearts of reader and influencer gatekeepers. Without your prioritizing, however, the rest of what I say won't matter much because you'll be too overwhelmed to do any of it.

Introduction to Winning the Hearts of Readers

Wrapping it Up

You can't do it all. Prioritizing in this area is critical to protecting your creative spirit and leaving you with enough energy left over to write, write, write.

- **Takeaway One:** Find the social media platform where you are most comfortable and where your readers most congregate and invest the majority of your promotional time and energy there.

- **Takeaway Two:** You don't have to go it alone. Team up with fellow authors in reader engagement and content production to share the burden and introduce yourself to their ready-made audience.

Stay with me. We're going to get into the nitty-gritty soon. But first, let's clear the air about some terms and misconceptions.

Chapter 28

Let's Clear the Air

Before I get further into this topic, I want to make sure we're all on the same page. I've been throwing out a bunch of terms that may not be familiar to everyone, so let's look at a few definitions—and a few misconceptions too.

Let's Synchronize Our Terminology

I think we all know what a reader is, but what do I mean when I talk about influencers? For instance, what are the differences between a reviewer, a blogger, and a Bookstagrammer? And what in the world is a BookTokker??

- **Influencers** are people who have the means and motivation to influence consumers to buy something based on their recommendation. The term 'influencer' can be a broad term that covers all the terms I mentioned in the previous paragraph.

- **Reviewers** read your book and post a review to retail sites, such as Amazon, as well as book discovery sites, like Goodreads and BookBub. They may also post their review to social media and a blog, but some readers don't have time or interest in wrangling those platforms.

- **Bloggers** have an established presence on a website from where they talk about (in our case) books. Book bloggers often write reviews, interview authors, and host giveaways. Sometimes they spotlight books without reviews but instead link up with other bloggers to feature a book in a weekly themed post such as Top Ten Tuesday or First Line Friday. In fact, you regularly can find both of these themed posts on ReadingIsMySuperPower.org. This alone can expand your book's reach, because an expected courtesy of the linkups is visiting other people's posts to see what books they are discussing too. Several bloggers, including myself, also do weekly update posts featuring Goodreads giveaways, blog tours, sales, book news, and the posts we did that week—doubling the likelihood that a reader will see your book on these blogs.

- **Bookstagrammers** are book lovers who specifically use Instagram as a platform to share about the books on their radar. Most of the time, they accomplish this through artful and creatively staged photos of a book or a stack of books. The visual appeal can be quite stunning and often has the 'I'm seeing this book everywhere' effect for book buyers. A growing component of Instagram influencing is also making reels, or short videos that are similar to what can be found on TikTok.

- **BookTokkers** are a rising group of influencers who recently have been taking the book world by storm. By utilizing the TikTok platform, they create short video clips that often incorporate funny voiceovers and catchy music with a few seconds of targeted images and/or text. These influencers have become the epitome of 'tiny but mighty,' when it comes to a small amount of content that packs a powerful punch in terms of generating sales. In fact, the other day I received a marketing email from a major brick-and-mortar retailer with the headline 'as seen on BookTok.' This is a platform to watch for its rapid growth. But it also has the potential to fizzle out just as quickly, much like BookTube did.

Clearing Up Some Myths

Now that we have a better grasp of the terms we're using, let's clear the air about a few misconceptions I hear from authors about readers and influencers. Too often, a few bad apples taint someone's opinion of the whole bushel, as my cowriters have also discussed in their chapters. We all understand this at a certain level, but sometimes we too easily forget it when we are weary of the publishing merry-go-round.

- **Myth #1:** Readers don't value books enough to pay full price for them.

Truth: If readers want a book badly enough, most of them *will* pay full price for it. Eventually. Like all consumers, though, we're hesitant to commit our budget-conscious spending to try an author we're not sure we'll enjoy. For self-published authors, this means that maybe you'll need to price the series starter eBook lower than the other books initially to get readers who then become invested enough to buy the others. Maybe you'll need to give away some preorder goodies to catch readers' attention at first. Traditional publishers may employ these ideas for their authors, too, where needed. But if you're writing the kind of stories, characters, and plot arcs that readers fall in love with, and you have the right influencers on your team, there will come a point when you won't have to wheedle a sale out of them through gimmicks or rock-bottom prices.

It is also worth noting that readers who aren't connected with authors and publishers on a conversational basis often don't understand the nuances of the industry or the cost involved in taking a book from idea to print. They see 'eBook' and think, "Well, they're saving on paper so why is it the same price?" We do the same thing at the grocery store, don't we? "I'm not paying this much for a bag that's more air than chips." Yet, there are reasons for that packaging and pricing and—circling back to my earlier point—if it's our new favorite brand of chips we'll probably buy it anyway. Collective industry time spent in increasing overall reader awareness of the costs of publishing might just pay off in the long run with a shift in attitudes toward pricing. Yes, some readers feel entitled to get all their books for free or 99 cents, but not all of us.

- **Myth #2:** Most influencers are just in it for the free books.

Truth: While that may have partially been why some of us started a blog or a Bookstagram account, the root cause for the right influencers was always to support as many authors and books as possible, even with a limited budget. Even though we do get free books as influencers, most of us still buy even more than we receive. With a little practice, you can discern the influencers who only want the free books from the ones who truly want to help authors. Phase out the first category once you've seen their true colors and invest in the ones—the majority—who are passionate about directing new readers to the books and authors they spotlight.

Some clues that an influencer wants all the freebies with none of the work can be found in their interactions with authors and on their platforms. Are they tracking *you* down to ask for a free copy instead of waiting for you to approach them with a review request? Do you notice them asking other authors for books, too, or complaining frequently on social media that they can't get print copies? Check their platform while you're at it. A blog doesn't have to be professionally designed, but does it look like it has just been thrown together with little or no consideration for quality? Or are they at least professional in their presentation? On Instagram, how are their book photos presented? Are most of their images lackadaisical and poor quality, showing minimal effort, or does it look like they are creative and thoughtful in how they present the books they feature? For blog and social media platforms, do they only feature the book for the promised post or do they repeat some books in list posts or book stack photos?

- **Myth #3:** Influencing isn't that time-consuming, and it pays well. Also, see myth #2.

Truth: Influencers who take pride in their work and want to show off their favorite books and authors with excellence work *hard*. This is a side hobby—a labor of love—for most of us, and we have other careers and responsibilities. Much time and effort go into maintaining our websites or social media feeds, responding to comments, sharing our blog posts on social media, writing a review, copying that review to multiple retail sites, creating graphics, keeping up with ever-changing algorithms, and generating fresh content.

This investment on our part is neither free nor remunerated. In addition to the large time commitment, some of us also pay a pretty penny for web hosting services and photo or graphic design apps. And while it's true that influencers for certain industries can make hundreds of thousands of dollars in sponsorships and advertising, the book influencing industry rarely pays anything more than a small handful of change from affiliate links. Don't get me wrong—we don't begrudge the way things are. We are honestly happy to make these investments because we are passionate about the books we love.

Let's Clear the Air

Wrapping it Up

Just like spending time to educate readers about the publishing industry can be helpful, it's also advantageous for all concerned parties when authors understand the time commitment and financial investment that influencers are making on their books' behalf.

- **Takeaway One:** Influencers make up a wide variety of platforms and practices, but ultimately, they use their reach to bring your books to the attention of their followers.

- **Takeaway Two:** Not all influencers are created equal. Learn to distinguish between those who just want free books and those who are truly hoping to make a difference for you.

- **Takeaway Three:** Dialogue with readers and influencers and help them understand the pricing structure for books. Also, remember that most influencers are not getting paid anything to promote your book and that, in fact, many are paying for the privilege to give you free marketing. Communication and education lead to greater understanding from both sides.

Influencers are a powerful marketing tool when approached correctly, and in the next chapter we'll look more closely at how to do that.

Chapter 29

The Care and Feeding of Influencers

After finding a batch of potential new readers, the next logical question would be how to approach them about reading and promoting your books. I'm mainly going to focus on influencers for a while because they are the gateway to the reader gateway, in a manner of speaking. The right influencer can get your book into the sightline of other readers in ways that no other marketing tool can, and it should cost you nothing but one or two copies of your book and maybe a bit of time.

We talked in the previous chapter about how to distinguish between the right and wrong kind of influencer overall. Now, I'm talking about finding the right influencer for *your* books. There are some excellent resources on social media to get you started.

Several influencers and authors have created Twitter lists comprised of other influencers (usually bloggers) that they recommend. Find an author on Twitter who writes in your genre and see if they have any lists for you to reference. Or simply look through the reviews and posts they have retweeted and follow the links to the influencers who are already spotlighting the kind of books you write. Another helpful trick on Twitter—and Instagram—is to search by genre-specific hashtags such as #contemporaryromance or #romanticsuspense to find readers and influencers who are talking about those books.

As I've mentioned previously, Facebook has a bevy of reader discussion groups for nearly every genre imaginable. Join a couple of active groups with like-minded readers and ask for some book recommendations related to your genres. Then, pay attention to the readers who give especially detailed or enthusiastic answers. Another option is to see if the group has files available for members, with lists of influencers and reviewers for you to contact.

Before you approach an influencer, however, a few minutes spent on the following tips will go a long way in establishing a positive relationship with them.

1. Give them time.

Most influencers I know, including myself, plan their review or posting calendars several months ahead. Chances are strong that, if you ask them to review your book before a release date that's only two weeks in the future, you're going to get a 'no.' We try to read all the books; we really do. Some of us have even made it our life's goal and are praying that books are the one exception to 'you can't take it with you.' No matter how fast we read, however, we need a reasonable head start to add your book(s) to our schedule. More on this in a moment.

2. Give them respect.

This may be one of the most important takeaways from this chapter. So often, my own first impression of an author has been determined by whether I can tell that they researched my blog before they contacted me. I know from talking with other influencers that they feel the same way, so this is a critical step in the care and feeding of those you approach to promote your books.

First and foremost, know their review and/or posting policies. Active influencers will have a page on their website or a highlight on their Instagram account with this information. These policies aren't just suggestions. We hope that authors will use them to learn helpful information such as how we want to be contacted, what books we are and are not interested in promoting, and our current turnaround times.

Then, respect those policies, especially if they give specific content guidelines. It doesn't do you any good to circumvent those preferences if you ultimately want to find the best match for your books. If they don't want to read or promote books with certain language, scenes, or themes, their audience probably doesn't either. Don't assume that your book will be the exception. In other words, please don't send a request to review your book about cowboy alien zombies in outer space to someone who reads only contemporary romance and romantic suspense. (Yes, that did in fact happen to a blogger friend.) You will get much better results if you practice a little patience and hold out for a blogger or Bookstagrammer who is passionate about the kind of books you write.

3. Give them information.

After the initial contact has been made and you are proceeding with plans for someone to feature your books, one of the easiest ways to make that influencer want to keep working with you is to provide them with any information you think they might need. Send them your media kit with current bios of various lengths to choose from, as well as your website and social media links. Include a high-resolution headshot and cover image too. We're going to delve into this more in a future chapter, but I didn't want to exclude it from this discussion because it's so helpful for influencers.

It's also helpful, particularly in our current culture, to make sure there are no surprises for readers as far as potential triggers or off-putting content. I certainly don't mean spoilers; please keep those to yourself! What I *do* mean, however, is that we like to know if a book has content that could possibly be offensive to the market in which you're promoting, or content that could bring up bad memories of past assaults, addiction, or abuse. If you're writing for the Christian fiction market, for example, give readers a 'heads up' if there are any curse words, intimate scenes (beyond kissing), or LGBTQ characters. If you're writing for the general market with a faith thread, it might be wise to at least drop hints to this end in the description. Be careful not to fall into the trap of listing every little thing that might bother someone—this is a guaranteed way to quickly go crazy. But, overall, if there is anything that has the potential to negatively surprise a *majority* of that genre's readers, it is to your advantage to let us know upfront.

4. Give them appreciation.

Remember that most influencers aren't getting paid for marketing your books and yet they are putting a lot of work into their posts. It's always nice when an author personally reaches out to thank us for a review or a post. When you share it in your networks, too, it makes our day. When you tell other readers or authors to check out our blog or Instagram account, we get an often-needed boost of encouragement and rejuvenation to keep doing our thing. Follow the influencers' blogs and social media accounts and interact with their posts about other authors, too, as you have time and mental stamina. Feature loyal readers and influencers in your newsletter or on social media. It extends our reach, which extends the reach of your book by default. Plus, it's just nice to know that someone appreciates what we are doing. We don't need tangible goodies all the time, nor do we need a bunch of fanfare on a regular basis. Occasional thank-you notes, messages or comments mean the world.

I'm often asked if authors should comment on reviews, whether positive or negative. My general rule of thumb is to answer in the affirmative with a few caveats. Yes, it's perfectly fine to thank a reviewer for reading your book and sharing their thoughts. In fact, most influencers love it when an author tells us they enjoyed a certain line in our review or a point we raised that others have missed. Don't feel like you must comment on every review, but if you want to thank a reviewer, please do! In another chapter, we'll be discussing how *not* to respond to reviews.

5. Give them grace.

Along with giving influencers enough time to plan a review or feature for your books, please give them grace if they need to change the date. Life happens, and I know very few full-time influencers in the book world. We have families, other jobs, health limitations, and that's not counting the wide range of situations that come up that are out of our control. Sometimes, too, we do take on more requests than we should have, and we get behind. Please give us grace when we tell you that we won't have the review up on time. Remember that no matter how dedicated an influencer appears to be, it's not a job we've been hired to do, but a hobby.

Wrapping it Up

Doing some easy research before you contact an influencer to promote your books will ensure that you are approaching the right kind of person and that you are showing respect for their hard work. Your books will find much more success if you take the time to match them to readers who love your genre and content.

- **Takeaway One:** Discover and respect an influencer's review and content policies to make sure your books are the best fit for them and their audience.

- **Takeaway Two:** Be free with your expressed appreciation for an influencer's work on your behalf, and be ready to extend grace when an influencer can't fulfill promised timelines.

Okay, but seriously, Carrie. What makes a reader try an author for the first time? Your patience will pay off in the next chapter, I promise.

Chapter 30

What Makes Readers Try a New-To-Them Author?

So far in our time together, we have talked about where readers spend time, how to filter out the kind of reader to pursue, and a basic overview of options when it comes to authors finding readers. I promised that we would do an in-depth focus on what makes a reader try an author for the first time, and here is where I make good on that promise. From aspiring to multi-published authors, this is the question that consistently is at the forefront of your minds.

Based on my experience, I can confidently tell you...

... There is no definitive answer.

Wait! Don't close the book in defeat. Stay with me. I promise that 'no definitive answer' does not equate to 'it's a lost cause.'

The reason it's difficult to give you clear-cut and concise steps to get your books in front of new readers is that the answer differs from reader to reader ... and from book to book, if we're being honest. What works for one book or author or reader may not work for the next.

Multi-published authors, this is probably not news to you. You and your publisher, agent, and editor have no doubt had similar conversations. Why does one book sell better than the rest? Why does a new author sell more copies of her book that released the same day as yours when you have an established readership?

I was recently doing research for a blog post on Seekerville about this topic, and I polled several of my blogging, reviewing, and avid reader friends to get their thoughts. Not surprisingly, there were as many different answers as people I asked. However, if we take the time to filter through the variety of answers, I think we can find some helpful common ground.

Survey Says …

As I read through the responses, I highlighted concepts that showed up more than once. Lo and behold, there *were* several repeated elements that these influencers said would entice them to try a new-to-them author. Things like:

- word of mouth
- recommendations from trusted readers
- social media
- book cover
- book blurb/subject matter/setting

Those commonalities may have been expressed differently per person, but, essentially, I found them to be saying the same things. Granted, each reader had unique answers too. But filtering out the minor differences and focusing on the shared responses instead helped me to zone in on the concepts that bring us closer to that elusive 'definitive answer.'

Then I got even more curious about what other readers would say. After all, the people I initially asked all read the same books, authors, and genres as I do for the most part. Would I get contradictory results if I polled a bunch of readers who have a wider range of preferences and aren't necessarily part of the blogging community?

I needed to know the answer. If I'm going to recommend that authors try these elements to get their books in front of new readers, I need to know that those bullet points go beyond book influencers. I wanted to make sure they stand true even when someone isn't inundated with books to review or immersed in the industry.

So, this time, I went straight to the vastest group of readers at my disposal—Facebook. I asked the same questions that I asked my initial influencers, and I waited eagerly for the answers. Would my list of repeated elements bear out with this wider audience?

Spoiler alert: it did.

Now, in the interest of full disclosure, most of the respondents were my friends and family, with the exception of people who found the question through another respondent's network. Knowing most of the people who answered was not a bad thing, though, because it gave me an advantage that most pollsters don't have. I'm aware of what they typically read—and don't read—so I can tell you with certainty that they did in fact represent a wide variety of reading habits and tastes. Out of 280 responses:

- 30.7 percent said **word of mouth** is what most causes them to try a new author;
- 25.6 percent said it was the **book cover or blurb**;
- 16.2 percent said they go by **reviews from trusted bloggers and/or Bookstagrammers**;
- 11.6 percent said that **social media posts** most influence them to try a new author.

As my spoiler alert indicated, each of those isolated commonalities points back to my initial polling of the smaller group. What does this tell us? Well, while it's not a definitive answer (because we've already established that there isn't one), it *is* a great platform to dive from when you swim in the 'what makes a reader try new books' ocean.

Perhaps you also noticed what I found to be intriguing—namely, that newsletters and reviews on retail sites do not seem to be dominant factors when readers decide to try a new author. The informal poll showed only 5.8 percent indicated retail site reviews were important to them, and only 1.4 percent said that newsletters helped with this particular decision. This is not to say that there is no value for either of these in an author's marketing strategy–Linda talks extensively about the benefits of building an email marketing list in her section. However, your newsletter's established readership and retail site reviews may not be as effective for the specific purpose of introducing those readers to a new author.

Do they have other benefits? Absolutely. After all, reaching that magical '50 reviews' goal opens doors to greater exposure on sites like BookBub and Amazon. Am I saying authors should ditch their email list or quit encouraging readers to review their books on retail sites? Absolutely not. I *am* saying, though, that most readers find new-to-them authors through word-of-mouth (including blogs and social media) and first impressions (cover/blurb).

Endorsements

Another result I found interesting is that, while I did not include it in my initial list of options, several people also wrote in **'endorsements'** as the most significant factor in trying a new author. Although endorsements could arguably be considered 'word of mouth' or 'recommendations from trusted readers,' I think they deserve a brief discussion on their own merit.

Spending a bit of time and, in some cases, money to develop professional relationships with well-established authors can give you a beneficial return on your investment when it comes time to getting endorsements that will make readers pick up your book. Go to those writers' conferences. Connect with local writers and meet together on a regular basis, whether in a formal chapter or an informal gathering at a favorite coffee shop. Join writing groups on social networks and engage in the conversations. Most popular authors I know don't have time to do many endorsements unless asked specifically by their publisher, agent, or editor. However, if you already have an established relationship with them, you will feel more comfortable asking them for an endorsement and, chances are, they will feel more comfortable agreeing to give one.

I know that's a lot of information and numbers, and if you're like me, your eyes start glazing over when math is involved. So, let me give you a quick summary that you can add to your author toolbox:

Wrapping it Up

When asked for the single most influential factor that causes them to try a new author, over seventy-five percent of polled readers pointed to 'word of mouth' (which includes social media posts and trusted reviewer recommendations) and 'book cover and/or blurb.'

- **Takeaway One:** Invest in (or insist on) a professional cover and get reader feedback on it and your back cover copy.

- **Takeaway Two:** Get that word-of-mouth machine working for you.

I already hear you asking, "But why? But how?" Let's look more at each of these takeaways in the next chapters.

Chapter 31

How To Make a Good First Impression on Readers

As the saying goes, you never get a second chance to make a first impression. For authors, this first impression can come in one of four main ways: the cover, the back cover copy (aka, 'the blurb'), the website, and personal contact (which we've already covered and will look at again later).

Books Are Judged by Appearance

We may say we don't judge a book by its cover, but our actions prove otherwise. It doesn't matter if a reader is browsing the shelves of their local bookstore or scrolling through a blog post or an online retailer, you've only got a second or two to grab their attention. While mankind looks at the outside of a person, God looks at the heart ... and readers look at the cover.

I'm not going to talk about the particular elements that are trending or outdated in cover design because they are too changeable. However, one thing I *can* discuss with some measure of knowledge is how the professionalism of a cover can make or break a reader's first impression. In my role as co-owner of a publicity tour company, I have seen time and again that the cover affects reader interest. If your cover doesn't reflect your genre or if it screams more 'you got what you paid for' than 'you know what you're doing,' I will face a much more difficult challenge in finding readers who are willing to review your book.

- **Research cover trends in your genre and follow them.**

If you oversee your own cover design and can control the final product, I can't emphasize strongly enough that your book cover needs to reflect your genre. If you are writing biblical fiction, for example, there are certain standard components that let readers know the genre before they even pick it up. Conversely, if your biblical fiction cover does not follow the norm, you will likely struggle to find the right readers.

To know that you're on the right track, you need to do some (here it comes again) research. This is the fun kind, though. Meander through your favorite bookstore and spend time among your genre's shelves. Grab a big stack of books and lay them out where you can look at their covers. Make a list of common elements, paying close attention to font style, colors, and images. Do they have a dynamic font or more of a script? Are there people on the cover or is it a setting? Is it a photograph or is it illustrated? Use what you learn in this step to make suggestions to your cover designer and hold out for them as much as possible. Keep in mind, however, that you don't necessarily want your cover to be a clone of all the others in your genre. You want your book to stand out among the crowd–for the *right* reasons, though.

- **Invest in (or insist on) a professional design.**

For authors responsible for their own covers, I realize that this costs money, but it has a much better chance of paying off in the long run than a cover that looks like a DIY project. If readers assume that minimal time or effort was spent on a cover's design, they may also assume that minimal time or effort was spent on the inside—namely, editing that story you want them to love. Much like curb appeal can either sell a house or keep it on the market indefinitely, a cover can either sell a book or leave it on the shelf. The cost invested in landscaping and adding some eye-catching features to a home's exterior is worth it when your home sells quickly and above the asking price. Likewise, investing money in a professional cover designer will be worth it when your book begins to make money for you because it has grabbed the attention of the right readers.

For traditionally published authors who have limited control over their final covers, it's still important to advocate for a professional and trending cover as much as you're allowed. If you aren't satisfied with the cover comps, speak up and ask if the problematic elements can be changed. The powers that be may not bend on the final cover, but they surely won't if you never ask. Publishers are on your side, and they want the book to sell well too. An initiated conversation can make sure everyone is on the same page and moving toward the same goal.

- **Reel them in with a well-placed hook.**

While you're spending time on the outside of your book, make sure your back cover copy is concise but also long enough to hook readers on the story. If the front cover catches a reader's attention, what do they do next? They flip it over and read the blurb. You've got their attention, but now you need to keep it. Don't waste a lot of time with superfluous information; instead focus on the plot hooks that will be most likely to convince readers to choose your book next. Make your blurb the bookish equivalent of the smell of fresh bread wafting from a bakery. Tug at their emotions, use key trope words (like 'mail-order-bride' or 'best friend'), and give them just enough information to make them hungry for more. It's also a good idea to run your book blurb—and your cover!—past some trusted influencers, readers, and even other authors. No, they likely aren't graphic designers or copywriters, but they *are* the people who will be buying your book.

Don't Let the Second Impression Cancel the First.

You've presented readers with a fabulous cover and an intriguing blurb. We'll talk more in another chapter about how to *keep* the readers you've hooked, but I can't overlook the importance of writing a good story. If their second impression of your work, the book itself, does not hold their attention, you will likely lose that reader right away. If you don't have the luxury of a publisher's team of editors, please make sure you hire an editor of your own. I am a cheerleader for many independently published authors and I understand the challenges, but when an author tells me that she is her own editor, I am much less inclined to read her book. When authors have studied their craft, have done the work to hone their God-given talents, and have allowed editors and critique partners to sharpen their writing, it shows. When they haven't, that shows too. Linda covered this wonderfully in her section, so I won't spend more time here.

Must-Haves For Every Author's Website

Authors can't always control their book cover or the blurbs, but they can control how their website looks and what content it contains. Picture this all-too-common scenario with me—I am doing a review for your debut novel, so I don't know much about you as an author yet. I search for your name on the interwebs, click the link it regurgitates at me, the website loads ... and ... I sigh with disappointment. I can find almost no helpful information I need to finish building my blog post. In fact, it doesn't even look like you want readers to connect with you at all.

What does this mean for you? Well ... if it's me on the other end of that click, it means that I'm going to scrounge up what I can find elsewhere because I'm stubborn. But an interested reader who looked up your website may get frustrated and go away, no longer invested in you or your books.

So, what are some basic, easy-to-do must-haves that *every author* should include on their website to tell readers and influencers everything they need to know?

- **Author Bio**

Ideally, you should offer a short bio and a medium-length bio on your website. Both options should be in third person. First person bios are just awkward for the influencer and don't sound as professional as those written in third person. My recommendation would be a maximum of three or four sentences for the short bio and double that length for the medium one. Also, please keep your bio updated. If I go to an author's website and her bio says something like "Her latest book releases in March 2017," but I am posting about her *actual* latest book that released in June 2022, I am going to be hesitant to use that bio in my post.

- **High-Quality Headshot**

You can have a variety of headshots to choose from or just the one. Quantity in this case is not as critical as quality. The photos you include should be high-quality and professional-looking. I'm not saying you absolutely must invest in a professional headshot (though I do recommend it) but at least make sure the quality is sharp and crisp. I also strongly suggest that your headshot shows you looking at the camera with a smile. Look friendly and open so that readers can imagine you saying, "Buy my book and you'll have fun." Why am I being picky about this? Graphics matter to influencers, and we need an image that stands up to the high-resolution graphics we make for our posts. We don't want to use pixelated, blurry, or stretched photos, because that reflects negatively on our own design work. Plus, an author photo sets a first impression for readers that, like the book cover, can reflect positively or otherwise on the assumed quality of your writing.

- **Updated Information**

This is related to what I discussed in the paragraph about author bios, but it also applies to your book information. Your latest release and your backlist should be easily discoverable on your website with high-quality front covers and a variety of purchase links. It's also not a bad idea to link to the publisher's page for your book. In other words, make it a piece of cake for people to find your books. (Now I want cake. And books.)

- **Social Media and Mailing List Links**

Basically, let readers know how to connect with you. If we love your books, we also want to follow you on social media, sign up for your newsletter, and learn more about you, your life, and what you're reading. If we find that we have things in common, then we're even more invested in you as a person *and* as an author. Personal connection with readers makes you an 'auto-buy author' for them, which translates into consistent sales over time. If they're coming to your website, they want to know more about you. Don't miss those opportunities!

Wrapping it Up

The key to making a good first impression on readers is to invest in outward focused elements that reflect the quality of the story you want them to buy. From the cover to the blurb to your website, each of these items needs to look professional and be designed to either hook or keep readers' attention.

- **Takeaway One:** Your book cover needs to reflect not only your genre but also the current trends for that genre. Consider investing in a professional design, because this really is the first impression your book gives to readers, and it can be worth the cost when done right.

- **Takeaway Two:** Get reader feedback on your book cover and book blurb, because it's not necessarily about what you like. It's about what readers like.

- **Takeaway Three:** Make sure your website has updated author bios, print-quality headshots and front covers, social media and purchase links, and newsletter signups in an easy-to-navigate design. For ease of use, combine them all into a media kit page.

With the all-important first impressions spiffed up and ready to go, you can use word-of-mouth to your best advantage. In the next chapter, we'll look at how to make it a successful marketing technique.

Chapter 32

How Do You Successfully Use Word-Of-Mouth?

A couple of chapters back, we analyzed an informal survey I did with almost three hundred readers. When asked what makes them try a new-to-them author, over 50 percent of the respondents indicated that word-of-mouth is most significant to them. This means it should also be significant to authors who want to woo readers.

Before social media, word-of-mouth existed in its most literal form—people talking face-to-face with someone else about a product or service they loved or hated. Today, it can occur in many forms, and we've already covered several of them. Readers, bloggers, Bookstagrammers, BookTokkers—each of these influencers builds and maintains his or her platform on this type of marketing. No matter how they share your books, it's their word-of-mouth that powers the promotion. Person-to-person recommendation is still of immense value, no matter the form it takes.

Sometimes, it's enough for you to organize your own word-of-mouth campaign. If you have the necessary time and energy to harness readers and influencers, giving them specific marching orders and making sure they follow through, go for it! I know authors who successfully do this all the time.

However, sometimes in prioritizing where your focus needs to be, you realize you need help in the word-of-mouth department. This is where a publicity tour company comes in handy. Companies like this help promote your books through a coordinated network of blogs and social media hosts.

Common Misconceptions About Publicity Tours

- **Myth #1:** Publicity tours should result in immediate sales.

Truth: While that would certainly be ideal, there are multiple factors that affect and influence book sales. A successful blog or social media tour should result in more *attention* directed specifically toward your book. Sales gained during the tour are a nice bonus. The tour company I started with my book sisters works hard to get Christian and 'clean read' books in front of people over and over and over again through our tours. Then, when readers see the book at an online retailer or in a store, they'll feel a connection to it and be more likely to buy it because they've seen it 'everywhere.' But this won't happen overnight. It's a cumulative process. A publicity tour should be another partner with whom you work to touch readers with your book as many times as possible.

- **Myth #2:** Blog tours are no longer effective. Podcasts are where it's at.

Truth: I would almost agree with that statement if it were for anything other than books. But books are for readers, and readers ... well ... read. While we might embrace a few podcasts that are relevant to our interests, we won't quit reading blogs or social media. Reading is at the core of what we do, and readers always want to know what books they should read next. Therefore, a blog tour or social media tour continues to meet readers where they are and potentially reach new audiences for your books.

How Authors Can Help Their Publicity Campaign Succeed

The tour company does the legwork and the managing of each tour so that you, the author, can focus less on marketing and more on writing delicious new books for us to read. But while we do most of the heavy lifting, there are some things authors can do to aid in achieving a successful word-of-mouth campaign from start to finish.

- **Plan ahead.**

Established tour companies who are at all successful in what they do are likely booked solid at least four months in advance. If you wait until January to request a tour for your February release (or, heaven forbid, your January release), you unfortunately will be out of luck. It's really never too early to plan your publicity campaign, but there is definitely such a thing as planning too late.

- **Don't put all your eggs in one basket.**

Ideally, you'll want to do a blog tour *and* a social media tour to keep the book popping up everywhere and staying on people's minds. BUT covers are key here. Some covers just don't work well on social media. It might be a great cover, but there are elements that get less engagement on social media. If your cover is dark, for instance, it's more difficult to find willing hosts. Covers with poor typography (not enough contrast with the color scheme, an unpopular font, too small or too large, etc.) and those with stock photos that are not properly integrated into the background also prove problematic for social media. Ask your tour coordinators for their recommendations and respect their expertise.

Allow me a word of caution for those who like to hire multiple tour companies to promote the same book. This practice can be useful to broaden the reach and audience for your new release, but it also has some potholes you'll want to avoid. These potholes are mainly caused by host overlap as most tour companies share at least some of the same hosts. Even though I own a publicity tour company, I also blog for several others. Many of our hosts also work with multiple companies in order to have the widest range of opportunities for books and authors to promote. If you do want to use more than one publicity company for the same release, it's best to use them for different types of tours. For instance, book a blog tour with one company and a social media tour with a separate company. It's also best to stagger the dates for each separate tour to avoid confusing the hosts and readership that overlap between the two groups. This also allows for maximum participation and a more focused campaign. As I mentioned in my first chapter, more is sometimes just 'more,' which makes it ineffective.

- **Have all your ducks in a row.**

I cannot emphasize enough how important this next statement is: Make sure your book is up on a platform like Goodreads and BookBub at least three weeks before the tour begins. If your book isn't on at least one of these sites, you are missing a vital marketing tool that costs you nothing. There *must* be a place for us to send readers who are interested in the book we're promoting. Retail site links are, of course, also vitally important, but the timing of those link visibilities sometimes doesn't match up with a promotional tour (with cover reveals, for instance).

The media kit I mentioned in the last chapter is also hugely helpful for the tour coordinators who are putting together materials for their hosts. It's also highly advisable to have an author Facebook page, separate from your personal timeline, for tagging and reach purposes. The algorithms just don't work the same way for a personal profile versus an author page.

- **Share and support.**

Share the tour posts on social media, if you have time, or at least share the giveaway info with a link to the company's landing page for your book's tour. An engaged author leads to a more engaged tour all around.

- **Just read.**

Okay, yes, this is a not-so-subtle nod to JustRead Tours, the company I started with my friends, but the principle remains true no matter who you've hired to promote your book on a blog or social media tour. Thoroughly read the invoice and all materials the tour company sends you. Important details and deadlines are often included in the invoice, terms and conditions, and 'next step' emails. If you have questions, don't be afraid to ask! That's what we're here for. Please do make sure, though, that you're aware of the terms you're agreeing to as well as the materials and deadlines that have been requested.

Blog tours and social media tours can be overwhelming, but these guidelines should ease some of the stress—for both you and the tour coordinators—and help your promotional campaign run as smoothly and productively as possible.

Wrapping it Up

Word-of-mouth is a significant element of marketing any product, and books are no exception. Invest in a blog tour or social media tour with a reputable tour company or start a grassroots campaign on your own to keep people talking about your book.

How Do You Successfully Use Word-Of-Mouth?

- **Takeaway One:** Manage your expectations. Successful word-of-mouth marketing requires consistent exposure over time.

- **Takeaway Two:** If you choose to work with a publicity tour company, plan ahead to get tour dates as close as possible to your book's release and thoroughly read all of the information, including the invoice, that the company provides.

First impressions have been made, and word-of-mouth has been engaged. How do you retain the new readers you've gained? I'm glad you asked! Let's talk about that next.

Chapter 33

Mostly Painless and Organic Reader Engagement

Wooing readers is not a one-and-done type of process. It requires an investment of your time and mental energy, and as we established at the beginning of my section, you must prioritize where you focus. In this chapter, I'll present several ways you can build reader engagement into your weekly to-do list, in hopes that you'll be able to find something that fits with your personality and comfort zone.

If you've been writing long, you know that some readers have no qualms about contacting authors. Unfortunately, these are often the readers who send nasty emails about why they didn't like your book or about the typo they found on page twenty-three. The readers you *want* to contact you—the ones who will encourage you, pray for you, and gush over your characters and wordsmithing—are sometimes just as intimidated to reach out to you as you are to reach out to them. They don't want to be a bother, or they are too busy fangirling to form coherent words. (Yes, I know this from personal experience. No, I'm not proud of it. Ahem.)

From my perspective as a reader, reviewer, and marketer, here are some simple action steps that even introverted or overwhelmed authors can take to increase authentic reader engagement and, at the same time, show they value us as part of their community.

- **Be active in bookish forums.**

As I've mentioned in other chapters, Facebook is great for this. The comment sections of popular book blogs or Bookstagram accounts are too. Join a few reader groups on social media that are active and have a healthy number of members. If you can't find any groups in your genre or market area (clean romance vs Christian fiction, for example), start one with a couple other authors or some influencers with whom you've already established a relationship. You can also do a Facebook search for popular books that are comparable to what you write, find people who are talking about them, and join them.

Readers and authors hang out in these places, and it provides a safe place to get your feet wet on this whole engagement thing. It's a comfier place for readers to reach out to authors as well. Seeing them 'in the wild' and realizing they love the same things we do helps us make personal connections that lead to our continued investment in that author's career. (Spoiler alert: By the time you finish reading this book, you will be saying 'connection leads to continued investment' in your sleep—if I have done my job correctly.)

- **Invest in a blog tour from a reputable publicity company.**

Didn't we just talk about this? Yes, we did, but I want to specifically highlight the benefits of a *blog* tour. I especially recommend them for debut or relatively new authors because typical blog tours include author Q&As and guest articles along with reviews and spotlights. These personalized posts allow readers to establish that all-important personal connection with the author which leads to future investment in that author's books. Even established authors can benefit from a blog tour because it exposes your books and brand to a different audience with each post. If you aren't sure where to look, get recommendations on publicity tour companies your author friends have used and loved. If a professionally organized blog tour isn't in your budget and you have a street team that works well for you, ask if any of the members would like to host you in a Q&A or guest post on their blog.

- **Approach interactions with your street team or reader group as building a community.**

If you treat your team interactions as something you 'have to' do or something to check off your to-do list, we can tell. I've been part of some street teams where the author only pops in to say, "I have a new book coming out. Here you go." I've also been part of street teams with authentic engagement between books, and I can tell the author truly cares about us as more than free publicity. I will give you one guess whose books I work the hardest to promote. There are many different ways you can accomplish this. Some authors share their prayer requests and praises with us, and they ask how they can pray for us in return. Other authors offer little snippets of their life, their travels, their writing progress, even their garage sale finds, and what God's been teaching them.

These authors tend to be favorites because they engage with their readers and, in doing so, make us feel a part of their community. When we feel like we are a part of what the author is doing, we are much more likely to become champions of the author as a person as well as an author. We love to support authors, and we love when authors let us know how to do so. Again, that authentic connection leads us to greater investment as readers because book marketing is more about building relationships than selling books. ('Community' will show up again at the end of this chapter.)

- **Start fun conversations on social media.**

This is easy to do and also provides you with insight into your readers. For example, one author friend asks engaging questions that correspond with various "National Days" such as National Strawberry Sundae Day or National Jigsaw Puzzles Day. A simple question is all that's needed, but you can also throw in an eye-catching graphic just to grab attention. Another author friend often chats about favorite books or romance movies, and she posts pictures of her beloved local mountains and a favorite historic home she loves to visit. Still another one posts about her intense dislike of discarded tooth flossers in random places, and now readers think of her whenever they see one. A unique and perhaps unintentional marketing angle to be sure, but it keeps her name in reader minds nonetheless!

You can find tons of icebreaker questions and bookish conversation starters online, so this is something that doesn't require a lot of thought, effort, or time. Just do it with some sort of consistency to keep the conversation going. If you go a significant amount of time without engaging your readers, you'll need to put in the work again to reestablish those connections.

Sometimes, though, life necessitates a break. It's okay to take the time you need, but I would suggest that you let your readers know you'll be on sabbatical. When you do return, find an easy way to sustain reader engagement for a while to regain any ground you've lost.

Why Community Matters

"Bookish folks should stick together. Bookish folks should all be pals. One may string the words together, but the other helps the stories sell." Dig deep into your imagination and pretend that little ditty I wrote was sung to the tune of "The Farmer and the Cowman Can Be Friends" from Rodgers & Hammerstein's *Oklahoma!*

Authors and readers can indeed be friends, even if only within the surface-level meaning of the word. If nothing else, we can connect over the obvious—our love of books—and if we're fortunate enough to connect through a shared faith, that bond becomes all the stronger.

From 2016 through 2019, I had a front row seat in watching these connections occur in special ways through the platform of the Christian Fiction Readers Retreat (CFRR). I also watched that connection lead to investment in both directions, and I've seen this unique community continue to grow into a family, in what I like to call 'the CFRR effect.'

Initially, the Christian Fiction Readers Retreat was supposed to be a brunch for a relatively small group of authors and readers. However, as the buzz for this event grew, so did the interest. My co-planners and I quickly realized there was a bigger need for this sort of connection than we had anticipated, and we needed to expand our plans accordingly. One hundred attendees and a full-day schedule later, we sat in awe of what God was doing.

Despite the imperfections that come with starting an event that is the first of its kind (and there were definitely imperfections!), feedback such as, "I've found my people," and, "I felt at home the moment I walked in the room," drifted our way. The next year's tickets sold out within thirty-six hours. Readers and authors alike craved this unique connection, and as they stayed in touch with their new acquaintances, a family began to form. This need for community could not be filled only by us, and there are now several other fabulous events that bring authors and readers of Christian fiction together in a family reunion of sorts.

This level of community has led to long-term and deeply personal author-reader relationships, and the resulting investment continues to provide opportunities for authors and readers alike. In all honesty, if I had not been involved in CFRR, I would not be writing this book, and I would have missed out on some of the most meaningful experiences in my professional life. Even more importantly, my personal life would be so much emptier without the precious friendships I made through CFRR.

Wrapping it Up

Reader engagement that is organic and winsome is essential to building a community of supporters who will stay invested in your career. Community matters. It leads to connection, and connection leads to investment. The lasting benefits of reader engagement are priceless—not just for your book sales, but also in having your own personal cheering squad when life and writing get tough.

- **Takeaway One:** The kind of readers with whom you want to connect can sometimes be intimidated to reach out to you too. Focus on engagement that feels natural to you and is fun to sustain long-term.

- **Takeaway Two:** It doesn't have to be complicated or too time-consuming. Build five minutes into your day where you make a conscious effort to make an authentic connection with readers over a shared interest or experience.

- **Takeaway Three:** Make 'community' a priority in your interaction with your readers. However, if you are only engaging us with 'buy my book,' that's not community. Community engages us with YOU.

We've talked about ways to hook and keep readers, and I've armed you with some easy tools for consistent engagement. After all this hard work, though, you want to avoid any landmines that might repel those same readers. So, let's examine some of the most common ones together.

Chapter 34

What Turns a Reader Off an Author?

We've spent quite a bit of our time together talking about those things that draw readers to new authors and keep them invested for life. However, one very important question remains unanswered. What makes a reader quit reading an author—or refuse to try them in the first place?

Just as the answer to 'what makes a reader try a new author' varies from reader to reader, so do the things that will turn a reader off an author. I asked several influencer friends to tell me their biggest peeves and turn-offs, and, as expected, I received a diverse sampling of answers. Once again, however, common threads showed up even in the differences. I want to spend some time on each one.

A Reader's Heart

Before I dig into these turn-offs, however, I want you to hear my heart—and the hearts of the influencers I polled. We want authors to succeed. We want their books to become buzzworthy bestsellers, and we want to do whatever we can to help them get there. When we know an author's heart in return, we are more than willing to forgive fleeting moments when perhaps she exhibits these turn-offs. We aren't perfect, and we don't expect authors to be either. That's the beauty of community, which we just discussed at length.

The purpose of this chapter is to be educational and constructive, not critical. These insights are offered from a heart who truly wants God's best for you. Maybe you've fallen into some of these traps and don't even realize they bother readers. Maybe this will be more of a cautionary tale for you instead. However it falls into your purview, I pray it will be received in the same spirit it is written.

Common Reader Turn-offs

No reader is created equal, and what bothers me won't bother someone else. However, the behaviors we're going to look at now are common buttons that authors shouldn't push.

- **Complaining about reviewers who won't review your books.**

This was one of the most prevalent turn-offs mentioned by the influencers I asked. In a previous chapter, we spent some time on the importance of showing respect for a reviewer's content preferences and turnaround time. This, though, extends beyond just the initial contact phase and your one-on-one interactions. It also applies to your conversations on social media and what you say to other authors or influencers about a reviewer. For example, one influencer told me about an author who frequently complains on social media that she has asked a blogger or Bookstagrammer to review her books and was told the reviewer didn't have time. Yet, the author sees this person reviewing other books and is personally offended. As that influencer said, "I would never purchase or read anything by her because she doesn't respect the reviewer's right to choose what they want to read within their time constraints."

Listen, it is humanly impossible for every reviewer to read every book that is presented to them. No matter how fast they read, it just can't be done. When a reviewer says she cannot review your book, even if it falls within that reviewer's preferred genre, it is usually because she is already scheduled to review thirty other books in the same timeframe. Or it may be that your book doesn't appeal to her. We try very hard to find that balance between the need to review everything we read and the need to protect our enjoyment of reading purely for the sake of enjoyment.

Sometimes, even when we have agreed to review your books, we can't fulfill our promises. In 2017, life derailed my review calendar. My father was diagnosed with stage 4 multiple myeloma (a blood cancer); my mother-in-law died from ovarian cancer only four weeks after her diagnosis; and I began rapidly losing my mobility due to a painful mystery illness that I now know was late-stage Lyme Disease. Grief, uncertainty, and fatigue dogged my brain and made reading for review difficult at best. In all honesty, it just wasn't as much of a priority as it had been when life was relatively easy. During that time, a couple of authors angrily expressed their hurt over my choice of some comfort re-reads instead of reviewing their books. I understand their perspective, and we still have friendly relationships, but I very rarely post anymore on social media about my recreational reading because of this experience.

Like the familiar quotation says, "Be kind, for everyone you meet is fighting a hard battle." Please don't take offense when a reviewer tells you they can't review your books but does review books by other authors. Remind yourself that you don't know what's going on in their lives or how many books they have already committed to read in the same timeframe. And surely you don't want them to review your book if they can tell it won't be a good fit for them. Also keep in mind that you are an influencer, too, and that your words have a reach you may not have intended. The community of reader and influencer gatekeepers is relatively small, in comparison, and we do talk to each other.

- **Complaining about reviewers who *do* review your books.**

Recently, from my perch on Instagram, I observed a disturbing interaction between an author and reviewer. I am acquainted with the reviewer through my tour company, but I only knew of the author through one of the influencer's recent negative reviews. While I understood the reviewer's mentioned concerns and respected her opinion, I personally did not feel that anything she addressed would negatively affect my opinion of this author's work. It was the author's own response that made certain I would never review or recommend any of her books. Her response to my acquaintance was hateful, full of anger, and, frankly, arrogant and immature. The best response would have been for her to say nothing at all or to leave a simple comment that said, "Thank you for your honest review. I'll take your concerns into account." By choosing to react rather than respond, this author lost at least two readers—probably more—and the potential reach of our combined audiences.

While that kind of extreme response is, in my experience, few and far between, there are more subtle ways that this shows up in author-reader interaction. I've fielded many complaints from authors about reviewers who gave their book no more than three stars, and I've heard stories of authors who have asked a reviewer to remove their review from retail sites. If the review has major spoilers or obvious signs that the reviewer didn't even read the book, I fully support the removal request. Beyond that, however, reviews are honest opinions that readers should be allowed to express.

Reviewing is admittedly a subjective process; after all, no two people read the same book the same way. We each bring our own biases, experiences, and preferences to every page written or every page read. When authors contact reviewers with requests to remove or edit unfavorable reviews, it puts us in an uncomfortable position and leaves a bad taste in our mouths for their books in the future.

- **Not supporting other authors.**

We love supporting authors who frequently champion books they haven't written. Reading is important to us (obviously), and we are drawn to anyone who can tell us what to read next. It tells us that you're a reader who knows the joy of being captivated by a plot, the way your heart skips a beat when you read a poetic turn of phrase, and the comfort found in familiar favorites. We then assume that your own books will be built on those page-driven experiences, and we start stalking the Internet for news of your next release. Conversely, when we see that you only talk about your own books, it leaves us to wonder if you have any of those reading experiences to draw from as you write.

Don't get me wrong—it's fine to promote your own books. We've just spent several chapters discussing how to do that very thing. It's when you *only* talk about your books that we may be turned off from reading your work in the future. Additionally, authors who write in one market (Christian fiction, for example) but never recommend books from that market raise our readerly red flags and make us question whether those authors even like their own market—which happens to be one we love.

Wrapping it Up

After tirelessly working to produce a well-written, professionally presented book that readers gobble up like ice cream on a hot day, the last thing you want to do is turn them away from you. Influencers and readers can be your biggest champions, but we all have our limits. It's a slow and often uphill climb to gain reader trust and investment, yet certain behaviors can instantly undo all the work you've already done.

- **Takeaway One:** Take a cue from Aretha Franklin and show R-E-S-P-E-C-T to the readers and authors you encounter in your writing journey. Be a prolific champion of both.

- **Takeaway Two:** Respond, don't react, to people who hurt you (intentionally or otherwise) in this industry. Better yet, don't respond at all. Check your frustration before you openly complain about reviews you don't like, reviewers who have offended you, or even other authors.

- **Takeaway Three:** Community plays a pivotal role in finding and retaining readers and often adds an extra cushion of grace to unchecked reactions. When your writing career becomes less about you and more about making lasting connections with other people, you will never lack for a loyal fan base or a built-in support network.

I have so enjoyed our time together, discussing how to get past the reader gatekeepers of the publishing industry. Before we say goodbye, I want to spend a few minutes talking about your story.

Chapter 35

Why Your Story Matters

Throughout this book, you have heard from four gatekeepers of the publishing industry with vital information for wooing the gatekeepers that we represent. However, all this material would be a waste of everyone's time if you walk away from this book wondering whether your story really matters anyway. I'm not talking only about the story you want to write, but also the story you want to live.

THE Story

I love story! I love short stories. I love epic stories. I love in-between-sized stories. I love contemporary stories. Historical stories. Mystery stories. Suspense stories. Amish stories. Even some speculative and young adult stories.

But most of all? I love THE Story, the one that starts with the ultimate 'once upon a time' (Genesis 1:1) and ends with the best 'happily ever after' ever (Revelation 21:4).

We are all part of that Story.

Yes, we all have a story in progress that is our own life. But everyone we meet does too. All these smaller stories are part of the Big Story that God is telling. That is SO exciting to me!

I never planned to write a book, and I still have no stories in my head demanding to be released. I'm content to read your stories and talk (incessantly) about them. But that up there? What I just said about being part of God's Story?

I am already part of the greatest Story in the world. And so are you. That's pretty stinkin' incredible. The Author and Finisher of my Faith is telling a Story about me and about you. He has promised to keep writing it until it's completed—not when I die or when you die, but until the day Jesus returns (Philippians 1:6). This has taken on new significance to me since my hero, my dad, passed away in December 2021. Suddenly, the promised 'happily ever after' where all the sad things become untrue seemed that much sweeter, and knowing that He is writing a Story that's bigger than I can comprehend was of vital importance.

You Are Not Alone.

In 2017, I had the pinch-me privilege of speaking with Cynthia Ruchti at the Art of Writing Conference in Nashville. We talked about the darts of author discouragement and how to dodge them. After our session, a woman came up to me in tears. She whispered, "I didn't know anybody else knew how I feel." We were both in tears after that!

Author friends, may I encourage you a moment? You're not alone. Writing may be a solitary career, but the discouragements are common. Fear of rejection. The *reality* of rejection. Fear of the inevitable bad review. The depths of despair over the bad review when it finally hits. Your family doesn't take you seriously. Your friends don't take you seriously. It doesn't pay the bills. It barely pays for coffee.

Wait, I was supposed to be encouraging you.

You're not alone. And you're not left defenseless.

God has given you each other, and He has given you His Word. Community and grace wrapped up in safe places like the readers who love your books and the authors who work alongside you.

Your Story Matters

Do you want to know another secret? YOUR STORY MATTERS.

Yep. I went there: all caps.

It's so incredibly true and so incredibly important to understand.

The story you're writing matters.

That story you've agonized over. The one that's kept you up all hours of the night. The one that may or may not currently be taunting you with a blinking cursor of 'I got nothing.' It matters. Even if no one else ever reads it. Even if no agent or publishing house wants it. Even if your beta readers and editors send it back with more tracked changes than you had words in the first place.

Your story matters. Believe it. And believe *in* it.

However, the story that God is writing in you and through you matters most of all. He is making you more like Jesus every day. He knew you before He formed you in your mother's womb, and He already had plans for your life (Psalm 139, Jeremiah 1). He created you as a writer before you even had fully developed hands to hold a pen or tap away on a keyboard. Even better—He knew your role in His Story before you were ever a consideration on planet Earth. And that story matters on a scale we can't even begin to imagine.

Maybe you're like me and the only thing you usually write is a blog post or a grocery list. Your story matters too. God placed you in His Story at just the right time and in just the right place so that you would come to know Him (Acts 17). He pursued you with an everlasting love and has engraved you on the palm of His hand (Jeremiah 31, Isaiah 49). Think about that for a second—you matter so much to the God of the Universe that those nail-scarred Hands have your name on them.

Your story matters. Believe it. And believe *in* it.

I know good stories. I'm surrounded by them, *à la* the Dr. Seuss method of decorating. All the crannies, all the nooks, etc. This Big Story that God is telling is a good story. It's the best story. It's the standard by which all other stories are measured, whether they realize it or not. It's also a *true* story. This fairytale to beat all fairytales—a prince on a white horse come to vanquish the enemy and rescue his bride—that's OUR story (Revelation 19).

Wrapping it Up

Wooing the gatekeepers of publishing to get your book published and in the hands of readers is a wonderful goal. However, there will come a time when every author is tempted to throw in the towel and give up on his/her story. When that happens, it's time to lean in to the Story that God is writing and let Him speak truth over you.

- **Takeaway One:** You are neither alone nor defenseless in the writing journey. God has given you a community of people to cheer you on, and He's given you His Word, inviting you to be part of THE Story with Him.

- **Takeaway Two:** Your story matters. Believe it. And believe *in* it.

THE END

Glossary of Terms

Acceptance: An official offer from a publisher to publish a book.

Acquisitions Editor: The editor who evaluations manuscripts from authors, negotiates contracts, and aids in the plans for producing the book.

Advance: A payment some publishers pay "in advance" of publishing a work. The advance is against future royalties, meaning that the author will not receive future payments until the advance is "earned out."

Amazon: The world's largest online retailer and a primary source for readers to purchase books.

Apex Hook: An Apex Hook is taking the pinnacle point of the story and turning that into the prologue. Then, in your first chapter, going back to a point before that event and leading your reader toward the Apex Hook.

Glossary of Terms

ARC (Advance Reader Copy): An early version of a book before it is published. ARCs may be sent as a hard copy or PDF format.

Author: Someone whose writing has been published.

Author-Agent Agreement: A legal document granting a literary agency the right to represent and promote an author's work. The contract includes language that will protect both the author and the agency.

Author Bio: A short description of the author, including their credentials for writing a particular book.

Author's Voice: A writer's style. An author's voice is the quality that makes one's writing unique.

Back Cover Copy: Text printed on the back of a book that describes the book's content. Back cover copy is often worded in a way to intrigue a reader to buy the book.

Backlist: A publisher's older books that are still in print.

Backstory: The history or background of a fictional character.

Best Efforts Clause: An agent promises to try their best to get a client a suitable publishing home for their book.

Bestseller: A book that has sold a large number of copies.

Big Five: The five large publishing houses that dominate the industry.

Glossary of Terms

Blog: Short for "weblog," a blog is an online journal that is updated frequently by an individual or group of individuals. Blogs are typically written in an informal, conversational style.

Blog Tours: A coordinated push of information about a book on various blogs, usually coordinated by a publicity tour company.

Blogger: A person who shares reviews, life vignettes, author interviews, guest articles, tips & tricks, lists, recipes, etc. from a website or blogging platform.

Blurb: The back cover copy that describes a book's plot and introduces the main characters to hook readers—not a full-blown synopsis.

Book Deal/Contract: A legally binding agreement between a publisher and an author that spells out the rights and responsibilities of each.

Book Launch: An event where an author celebrates and promotes the release of a new book.

BookBub: A free service that helps readers discover books they will like by reading recommendations from other readers.

Bookseller: A proprietor or business that sells books, either online or in a brick-and-mortar setting.

Bookstagrammer: A book lover who specifically uses Instagram as a platform to share about the books on his/her radar, usually through artful and creatively staged photos.

Glossary of Terms

BookTokker: A book lover who specifically uses the TikTok platform to create and share video snippets about books and the bookish life.

Brand: An author's brand is what readers expect from an author. Branding "tells" potential readers why your books are a good fit for them.

Byline: A line that names the writer of an article.

Campaign: An email or sequence of emails sent to multiple recipients at one time with the purpose of providing valuable content and a relevant offer.

Chapter Outline: For nonfiction projects, a summary of each chapter in a book. Some fiction publishers also request a chapter-by-chapter outline in addition to a synopsis.

Character Arc: A character's inner transformation over the course of a story.

Checking In: Asking a publisher or agent for an update on a submission.

Chicago Manual of Style: An American English style and usage guide considered the standard for U.S. style in book publishing.

CIP: Cataloging-in-Publication data is useful for certain books, especially nonfiction, and will ensure a book is shelved correctly in libraries. CIP data is not typically necessary for genre fiction.

Cliffhanger: An ending to a writing segment that leaves the reader in suspense.

Comparative Titles: Titles that have been published in the last five years, in your genre, that are similar to your book. Comp titles help the agent or editor understand your book's place in the market.

Content: Materials, such as images, videos, audio recordings, or text that is posted or shared, typically through newsletters or social media channels.

Contract: A legal agreement between an author and a publisher that may involve a single written work or series of work.

Copy Edit: An edit that includes checking an author's work for grammar, spelling, punctuation, and style in order to prepare the work for the final proof.

Copyright: A copyright gives the owner exclusive rights to copy, distribute, or adapt a creative work.

Cover Letter: A formal communication between an author and either an agent or the editorial staff of a publishing company. A cover letter is typically included in the initial submission or query.

Craft: A writer's craft consists of elements that make stories readable, including good grammar and usage as well as (for fiction) plot, characterization, pacing, dialogue, structure, and point of view.

Critique: A critique is an analysis of a piece of writing that includes descriptions of the writer's strengths and weaknesses.

Debut Novel: The first work of full-length fiction an author publishes.

Glossary of Terms

Development Edit: A phase in the editing process where a thorough evaluation of the manuscript is conducted to determine what revisions are necessary to prepare the work for publication.

Dialogue: A conversation between two or more people, typically used when referring to written works.

Distributor: Book distributors sell titles to bookstores, retailers, and libraries.

DM (Direct Message): Sending a message to an agent or publisher on social media, hoping to bypass the standard submissions process.

"Earn Out": When a book "earns out," it means enough copies have sold for the publisher to recoup the advance paid to the author.

Editor: A person who prepares a manuscript for publication by assisting the author with revisions, correcting spelling, grammar, and fact checking.

Elements of Fiction: The elements of fiction include plot, setting, characters, point of view, theme, tone, and style.

Elevator Pitch: A brief description of a book idea that explains the concept in a short period of time.

Feedback: Any comments or suggestions given to a writer with the purpose of helping a writer make revisions to a manuscript.

Fiction: A creative narrative work about persons, places, or events created from the author's imagination, often referring to novels, novellas, and short stories.

Glossary of Terms

First Reader: A person who reads a book as the author writes it, giving feedback and suggestions before anyone else sees it.

Flashback: A scene or section of a scene that takes place before the main narrative.

Fleshed-out Character: One with enough substance to make that character seem real to the reader.

Followers: When referring to social media, followers are users who have subscribed to receive a specific type of content, such as posts on Twitter, Instagram, Facebook, etc.

Format: Manuscript formatting includes elements such as font, font size, font styles (such as bold and italics), paper size, line spacing, paragraph breaks, and anything that contributes to the document's visual appearance.

Freelancer: A person who is hired to perform a specific task without a long-term commitment to any one employer.

Frontlist: A frontlist is a list of the publisher's recently released titles that are expected to sell better than average.

Full: When an agent requests to see your entire manuscript, that is called requesting the "full." Unless you write adult nonfiction, ensure you have your whole manuscript finished *and* polished before you audition for agents.

Galley: A preliminary version of a manuscript used by authors, editors, and publishers, typically used for proofreading purposes.

Glossary of Terms

Gatekeeper: Anyone in a position to accept or reject a manuscript, such as a literary agent, an acquisitions editor, and a publisher.

Genre: A category of books characterized by similarities in form, style, or subject matter.

GoodReads: A website community for readers to seek book recommendations and leave reviews.

Guidelines: Rules set by a publisher that explain the type of submissions they are accepting for consideration as well as how to submit manuscripts. Publishing submission guidelines typically include preferred genres, manuscript length, formatting, and what to include in a proposal.

Hashtag: A word or phrase (with no spaces between words) preceded by the pound sign (#), used to filter social media content by topic.

Headshot: A professional portrait of one person to be used on the subject's website and/or social media profiles.

High Concept: A book (or movie) with an easy-to-grasp premise that appeals to a wide audience. High-concept books can often be summed up with a single iconic image or a catchy tagline.

Hook: The hook is a story's opening that grabs the reader's attention and entices them to keep reading.

Head Hopping: Switching between more than one point of view within a single scene.

Hybrid Publishing: Often referred to as self-publishing assistance, author-assisted publishing, or co-publishing, hybrid publishing is a partnership between the author and publisher that combines elements of both traditional publishing and self-publishing. Hybrid publishing models vary, but in most cases, the author covers some or all of the publishing expenses, such as editing, formatting, cover design, and has greater creative control plus keeps a higher percentage of the royalties.

Imprint: An imprint is a brand established by publishers to identify a line of books geared toward a specific segment of the market.

Indie Publishing: Although this term initially referred to independently owned publishing houses (i.e. small presses), in recent years it has come to mean publishing a book without going through a traditional publisher.

Influencer: A person who has the means and motivation to influence consumers to buy something based on his/her recommendation

IngramSpark: An online publishing platform that enables self-publishers and small presses to print, globally distribute, and manage print and eBook titles.

ISBN: The International Standard Book Number is a numeric commercial book identifier. Each separate edition and variation (paperback, hardcover, eBook, and audiobook) has a unique ISBN.

KDP: Launched in 2007, Kindle Direct Publishing is Amazon's publishing platform, used by self- and traditional publishers.

Keywords: Words and phrases used to describe the content of a

Glossary of Terms

book. Keywords (and metadata) are what make your book appear in online searches when a reader types in specific search terms.

Launch: A book launch is a promotional strategy that includes all the planned marketing activities surrounding the release of a new book. A launch may include a specific event, such as an online launch party or an in-person book signing.

LCCN: LCCN stands for Library of Congress Control Number and is a unique identification number assigned by the Library of Congress for titles it will acquire.

Lead Magnet: A free item or service given to someone who subscribes to a newsletter or marketing email list. Marketers often refer to a lead magnet as "an ethical bribe," because it is used to entice website visitors to join their list.

Lead Time: The typical time it takes for a book to go from contract to publication. For most publishers, the lead time falls between nine months and two years.

Line Edit: A line edit, often confused with the term "copy edit," is the process where an editor goes "line by line" to tighten sentence structure. In fiction, a line editor may work scene by scene, paragraph by paragraph, line by line.

List: Names and email addresses of persons who have subscribed, usually via a website form. When a publisher or agent asks about the size of an author's list, they want to know the number of subscribers.

Literary Agent: An advocate for an author who will present their manuscript to a publisher, negotiate contracts to ensure the author gets the best deal possible, and serve as a mediator between the author and the publisher. Most large publishers only accept book submissions from literary agents.

Manuscript: Derived from the Latin term *manu scriptus*, which means "written by hand," today the term manuscript refers to the unpublished draft of a novel, short story, or nonfiction book.

Marketing: Book marketing consists of a series of promotional activities, events, and tasks to bring about an awareness of a book to readers and booksellers.

Marketing Plan: An extensive plan to get your book in front of the right audience, at the right time, and within a specified budget.

Mass Market: A mass market paperback (MMPB) is a book format where the title is produced in a smaller size, often with low-quality paper for the pages and cover, compared to a trade paperback edition, to keep printing costs down.

Media Kit: A collection of an author's bio, social media links, headshot, covers, and other information that would be pertinent to influencers and members of the media.

Metadata: Any relevant information that describes a book, including title, subtitle, ISBN, publication date, price, genre, keywords, etc.

MG: Short for Middle Grade. MG books are written for ages 8-12 and are generally 30,000-50,000 words in length.

Midlist: A list of a publishing house's recently released titles that are expected to have average sales.

Glossary of Terms

Ms: Short for manuscript. Mss is plural (manuscripts).

Newsletter: A newsletter is a regularly delivered email to an author's readers and prospective readers. This email is sent to those who have signed up (also called "opted-in") to receive news and updates from the author.

Nonfiction: Writing based on actual events and/or people that is based on facts.

Novel: A book-length fiction narrative.

Novelist: One who writes novels.

Novella: A short novel or a long short story. Novellas typically run between 10,000 and 40,000 words.

Onboarding Sequence: A series of emails sent to a newsletter email marketing list that introduces a new subscriber to the author's content. This sequence is emailed automatically through triggers configured by the list owner or manager.

One Sheet: A single sheet of paper that shares critical information about a manuscript, such as word count, genre, etc., as well as the author's bio.

PA (Personal Assistant): A person hired to help an author with marketing and/or other tasks.

Pacing: Pacing refers to how slow or fast the story moves for the reader.

Glossary of Terms

Partial: When an agent requests to see part of your manuscript. The agent will specify what this means. It can be anything from the first three chapters to the first fifty pages.

Pen Name: A name a writer uses on published works instead of using their actual name.

Pitch: A pitch is a brief description of a story intended to convince an agent, editor, or publisher to accept the piece.

Pitch Party: A Twitter event where writers who have a completed, unagented manuscript can tweet their book pitch using hashtags to designate genre, target age, and other information as specified by the party's organizer.

Platform: A writer's ability to market their work, using their overall visibility It's a quantifiable number, and often involves pulling sales data, social media numbers, and speaking engagements.

Plot: In fiction, a plot is a sequence of events that make up a story's narrative. A basic plot includes an exposition or setup, rising action, climax, falling action, and resolution.

POD (Print on Demand): A printing technology where books are printed only when an order is received by a company. This allows for the printing of single copies or small quantities.

Point of View (POV): The perspective from which an author tells a story.

Print Run: The number of copies that a publisher will have printed of a forthcoming book.

Glossary of Terms

Promotion: Book promotion (or promo) is the process of convincing potential readers to buy a book.

Proofread: The act of reading an edited manuscript and annotating mistakes. Proofreaders typically look for errors that involve spelling, grammar, usage, and spelling.

Proposal: A document that explains why your book is marketable. Some sections in this proposal include author bio, platform information, comparative titles (books published in the last five years, similar to yours), marketing plan, a synopsis (fiction) or chapter outline (nonfiction), and the first three chapters.

Pub Board: A meeting of publishing company professionals who make the final determination whether or not to publish a book.

Publicist: A person who generates and manages publicity for a book and/or author.

Publicity Tour Company: A company whose ultimate purpose is to spread the word about products or services (in our case, books) by coordinating a focused group of influencers to share the book on their platforms and increase exposure for the book and author.

Publisher: A company that publishes the book of an author—whether via a physical paperback/hardcover book, digital book, audio book, or a book in any form.

Query: A cover letter for your proposal. No longer than a page, this letter tells an agent or acquisitions editor what the book is about, why it's a good fit for the agent or publishing house, and why you are the best person to write it.

Querying: Submitting a query letter or proposal to a publisher or agent for consideration.

Reels: Short, attention-catching videos created specifically for social media.

Rejection: When an agent or publisher passes on a proposal or manuscript that has been submitted to them.

Reporting Time: The time an agent or acquisitions editor takes to respond to submissions.

Requested Materials: Documents an agent or acquisitions editor has requested that you submit to help decide whether to accept or reject a manuscript. Requested materials may include a proposal, sample chapters, information about the author, or the full manuscript.

Returns: Unsold copies of a book that a retailer may either return to the publisher or destroy. The publisher absorbs the cost of returns.

Reviewer: A person who reads and reviews books (or another sort of product or service) and then shares that review on retail sites, social media, and/or blogs.

Revise and Resubmit: If an acquisitions editor or an agent sees potential in a manuscript that isn't ready for publication, they may request the author to make revisions and resubmit the revised manuscript. Some editors and agents will make suggested changes.

Rights: A standard book contract grants a publisher the right to publish the book. There are two types of rights: Primary and Subsidiary. Primary rights establish the type of publication, such as print and electronic format. Subsidiary rights include the right for a publisher to make adaptions of the book, including audiobooks, foreign translations, etc.

Royalties: An agreed-upon amount of money a publisher pays the author in exchange for the rights to publish a book. Royalties are disbursed at intervals specified within the publishing contract.

Sample Chapters: Chapters from the actual manuscript that are included in a book proposal.

Scene: A scene is a segment of a novel that introduces a goal, conflict, and disaster. Effective scenes reveal the actions, emotions, decisions, and dilemmas of a character. Think of a scene as a mini story, with a beginning, middle, and end without a change in time or location. Scenes are written from the point of view of one character.

Self-publishing: Production of an author's work without the involvement of an established publisher.

Shotgun Submissions: Sending a form query to multiple agents in the same email, hoping one of them will respond.

Simultaneous Submissions ("Sim Subs"): Queries or proposals sent to more than one agent or acquisitions editor at the same time.

Slush Pile: Unsolicited manuscripts that have been submitted to a literary agent or acquisitions editor for publication consideration.

Small Press: A traditional publisher with annual sales below a certain level or below a certain number of titles in print. In the United States, a publisher with annual sales below $50 million or one that produces less than ten titles per year is considered a small press.

Glossary of Terms

Social Media: Community-based websites and applications that enable users to share and create content and interact.

Social Media Tours: A coordinated push of information about a book on various social media platforms, usually coordinated by a publicity tour company.

Story Arc: The plot line a story follows from beginning to end

Street Team: A group of fans who voluntarily "hit the streets" to spread the word about an upcoming book or product.

Style Guide: A style guide or style sheet is a set of standards for writing, editing, and formatting documents for a specific publishing house. Most trade book publishers use the *Chicago Manual of Style* but may also add house-specific elements.

Submission: Documents sent to a literary agent or acquisitions editor to request representation (by an agent) or, when sent to an editor, publication.

Subscriber: A person who agrees to receive email updates from a newsletter or marketing list, usually through a website signup form.

Subsidiary Rights: Any rights outside of a physical paperback or eBook. A publisher may ask for such rights as audio, TV, stage play adaptations, and more.

Subsidy Publisher: Also known as fee-based publishing or a vanity press, subsidy publishers require authors to pay an upfront fee to publish and market the author's book. Vanity publishing differs

Glossary of Terms

from self-publishing assistance in that the fees are often inflated and packages may include services an author doesn't need.

Subtitle: A phrase following the main title of a book to give it more context.

Synopsis: A single-spaced summary of what happens in your fiction manuscript from start to finish.

Target Audience: In writing, a target audience is the demographic an author expects will read a book. Factors considered when determining a writer's intended audience include age, location, culture, education, and genre preference. Simply put, a target audience answers the question, "Who is this book written for?" Or "Who will be most entertained (for fiction) or helped (for nonfiction) by reading this book?"

Termination Clause: An agent or publisher clearly spells out how the client or author may terminate their contract prior to or after publication.

"The Call": An interview between the author and the agent to decide if they would be a good fit for one another.

Title: The name of a published work, usually selected by the author, although publishers may change the title.

TOC (Table of Contents): A list placed at the front of a book that lists its chapter and/or section titles.

Trade Paperback: A high-quality softcover edition of a book.

Glossary of Terms

Traditional Publishing: The production of a book by an established publishing house where the publisher pays for all the expenses and disburses a percentage of the book's earnings to the author as royalties.

Unagented Submission: A proposal or query from an author who does not have a literary agent.

Unsolicited Submissions: An unsolicited submission means no one from a literary agency or publishing house has requested to receive the submitted materials.

Vanity Press: See Subsidy Publisher.

Virtual Assistant (VA): A virtual assistant can help authors with marketing, social media, administrative tasks, blog management, and more.

Website: Simply put, a website is a set of related online pages published under a single domain name, usually by one person, business, or organization.

WIP/Work-in-Progress: An incomplete manuscript.

Word-of-Mouth: The spread of information, specifically product recommendations, through conversation, blog posts, and/or social media

Writers' Conference: A conference in which industry professionals can take pitches from writers. At these events, authors can also sit in on classes that teach them up-to-date information about the industry.

Acknowledgments

From Hope Bolinger:

To my Lord and Savior Jesus Christ who has opened doors in publishing when I thought they were shut.

To Linda, who graciously spearheaded this project after I told her about a class I taught at a conference.

To my agent Tessa, and to all the industry professionals who have helped me to rear my books and bring them into bookstores.

To the magnificent people who are working on this book.

To the brilliant three other authors who I have the pleasure of working with, to help elucidate the publishing world more to readers.

And to the readers who have picked up this book. I hope this has been helpful in your writing journeys!

From Linda Fulkerson:

God had His hand on this project from the beginning, and all glory goes to Him for seeing this book through to completion.

I want to thank Liz Johnson for inviting me to participate on the faculty of the 2022 Write to Publish Conference. Without the dedication of Liz and Jane Rubietta, this book would have never come to be, because that conference is where Hope presented a class on this topic, and that's where I told her I thought her concept would make a great book.

Thanks to my Scrivenings Press family, the most supportive team

I've ever worked with. You pitched in to help when asked. Waited on me when I ran behind. Never complained. I'm so blessed to be part of this company!

To my daughter, Dr. Elena Hill—thanks for being my sounding board not only throughout this project, but in life. I'm more proud of you than you could ever imagine.

A special thanks goes out to all who endorsed this book and to our beta readers for helping catch things we missed.

Finally, thanks to my co-authors for pulling together to create this great resource for our fellow writers.

From Rowena Kuo:

So many have been with me throughout my publishing journey. I would like to thank my brother, Roger Gualberto, and my mom, Lourdes "Lou" Gualberto. My children, Brandon, Lianna, Logan, and Evie, you will always be my inspiration. Ed Johnson, thank you for pointing me in the right direction. Kristine and Dale Hansen, I will never forget you for believing in me. Meghan Burnett, my business partner in the publishing world, let's publish great books forever. Cecil Murphy, thank you for the scholarship that started it all. Lin Johnson and Marlene Bagnull and all the conference directors who have invited me to grow and teach with you, I have enjoyed every moment. Eddie Jones and Cindy Sproles, I am grateful for years we worked together. Hope Bolinger, Linda Fulkerson, and Carrie Schmidt, thank you for writing with me and including me in this great work. Wayne, Austin, Aria, McKenna, and AKB, thank you for adopting me into your family.

To my colleagues in publishing and film, you helped me every step of the way.

And I thank the Lord Almighty, Who makes all things possible.

From Carrie Schmidt:

First and foremost, Jesus—You have been my Best Friend since I was a little girl. You have sometimes been all I had, and You're always everything I need. Thank You for making 'story' the language of my heart and for allowing me to play a small role in Your Story. You have the words of Life.

Mom and Dad, thank you seems ridiculously inadequate, but it's the best the English language offers. You bought me books (and bought me books) and read them to me, then read them *with* me. You were my first (and loudest) cheerleaders, encouraging my imagination and my love of story at every turn while pointing me back to Jesus as the best Author. Dad, I miss you more every day. Even your dad jokes. Mom, I've been so proud of you this year, and I know Dad would be too (after all, HMAB). If God put alllllllllllll the parents in the world in one big room ... (you know the rest).

Eric, how many people are blessed to fall in love with their best friend, without even trying? To marry someone who makes them laugh every day? To know their spouse was hand-picked for them by a grinning roommate and a list-making grandma? To have a partner who doesn't mind a house that could double as a library (except maybe when moving to a new house)? I love you, BB, and I'd choose you all over again. Thanks for tolerating my book boyfriends and my crush on Joe Kenda.

Josh, you were one of my first answers to prayer – the baby brother I asked for and knew I would get, even when no one else believed me. You have stretched me out of my comfort zone more than anyone else, and I love you all the more for it. Thank you for loving me as I am but also for always challenging me to be better.

Carrie and Sherrie—my 'ride or die' sisters since the second grade. God gave me two of you because He knew this kind of friendship, our cord of three strands, would be impossible to duplicate otherwise. Thank you for praying with me and for me, for reminding me of His Word, for loving stories with me, and for always being friends with whom I can be fully myself. Happy birthday, Pam!!

Bonnie and Annie, thank you for inviting me to help with the 'just a small brunch' that turned into the Christian Fiction Readers Retreat. I can't put into words how building that community with you changed my life.

Melony Teague, thank you for loving me as me, for your precious-to-me friendship, and for sitting with me in my grief this year. Pepper Basham, thank you for being my first author friendship, for speaking your wisdom over my life, and for giving us squished grandpas, closet kisses, and Grace. Carla Laureano, thank you for creating #myJames because, along with being super swoony, he helped me find my brand and my voice. June McCrary Jacobs, thank you for your faithful prayers for me and my family—I'm so blessed to be your friend. Beth and Rachel, thank you for being my book sisters and my partners in just about everything—I can't imagine doing any of the last few years without you. I love you all.

My cowriters—Linda, Rowena, and Hope—thank you for inviting me to join you for this book project. I am so honored by and grateful for the opportunity to share my heart.

And finally—Keegan, Deitrich, Eloise, Michaela, Steven, Delaney, Noah, Jayla, Isaac, Benjamin and Bear, I love being your aunt and I love now being in such close proximity with almost all of you after being a long-distance aunt for much too long.

To every author whose books I've ever read, thank you for entertaining me for over 40 years. Your story matters.

About Hope Bolinger

Hope Bolinger is an acquisitions editor at End Game Press, and a former literary agent. She is also the author of 20+ books, and has 1400 of her other works in print in various publications. When she isn't busy accidentally writing a book in a week, you can find her doing local theater, modeling on runways, or getting lost in the Ohio metroparks. Find more about her at hopebolinger.com.

About Linda Fulkerson

USMC veteran Linda Fulkerson began her writing career as a copyeditor and typesetter at a small-town weekly newspaper. She has since been published in several magazines and newspapers, including a two-year stint as a sportswriter and later the online editor of a midsize daily. Linda also served as the director of digital services for the largest media outlet in central Texas. She is the author of two novels, two novellas, and several nonfiction books. In 2020, she founded Scrivenings Press LLC, a traditional publisher of clean and Christian books.

Linda and her husband, Don, live on a ten-acre plot in central Arkansas. They are part of an RV ministry group and travel the country volunteering at various entities. Linda and Don have four adult children and eight grandchildren. In addition to kicking back in her recliner with a good book, Linda enjoys photography, travel, and spoiling her two dachshunds.

About Rowena Kuo

Rowena Kuo is the CEO and Executive Editor for Brimstone Fiction, Brimstone Books and Media, and Brimstone Fire. With over 15 years of ministering to children, youth groups, young adults, women, and family groups, Rowena advocates for writers to build God-centered support systems consisting of people, perseverance, practice, and most of all, prayer. She has written for Christian Devotions, Written World Communications, Splickety, and the 168 Write of Passage. When not working on words or films, she is a full-time mom with secret aspirations for spaceflight.

About Carrie Schmidt

Carrie Schmidt is an avid reader, book reviewer, story addict, KissingBooks fan, book boyfriend collector, and cool aunt. She also loves Jesus and THE Story a whole lot. Carrie started the popular blog ReadingIsMySuperPower.org in 2015 and since then has had the honor of co-founding the Christian Fiction Readers' Retreat and JustRead Publicity Tours. In addition to these endeavors, she is a regular contributor to Seekerville and has written for magazines such as *RT Book Reviews* and *Christian Market*. Carrie now lives in Georgia with her husband, though her roots range from East Tennessee to Central Kentucky and northern Illinois. You can connect with Carrie on ReadingIsMySuperPower.org, Facebook @meezcarriereads and everywhere else social at @meezcarrie.

Get Free Stuff!

Join our email community and get a FREE tip sheet to help you get past the publishing gatekeepers. You'll also get periodic exclusive content, updates, and special offers.

Visit this link or scan the QR Code to join now!

https://gatekeepers.link/join

INDEX

Index

Symbols
3-Act Story Arc, 144

A
About the Author, 84, 96, 172
Acknowledgements, 40
Acquisitions Editor, 40, 60, 77, 79, 99, 141–144, 146–152, 174
Action, 144, 156, 159, 161–162, 165, 167, 221
Active, 113, 156, 167–168, 183, 185, 196–197, 222
Advance, 32, 38, 71–72, 99, 104, 217
Advanced Reader Copies, 112
  ARC, 144, 148, 151, 158
Advertising, 114, 193
Advice, 30, 68, 85, 95, 99, 132–133
Agency, 24–25, 27, 29–34, 40, 42–43, 48, 55–57, 60–62
Agreement, 24, 26–27, 30–31, 33–34, 38, 60, 66
Agreement Duration, 30
Amazon, 66, 73, 80–81, 90, 107, 118, 171–172, 190, 204
  Amazon's Algorithm, 81
American Dream, 147
Anchor Author, 187
Apex Hook, 158, 162
Art of Writing Conference, 234
Aside, 160
Aspiring Author, 69, 78, 124, 127
Atticus, 106
Audiobook, 104
Austen, Jane, 180
Author Legacy, 179
Author Platform, 66, 81, 95, 98, 115, 118, 122
Author Website, 79, 118
Author XP, 186
Author's Career, 40, 84, 222
Author's Voice, 139, 144, 146–148, 150–151, 156, 179
Aweber, 116

B
Back Cover Copy, 96, 171–172, 205, 207, 209
  Blurb, 94, 171, 202–205, 207, 209–210, 212–213
Backlist, 212
Backstory, 159–162, 179
Bad Review, 234
Baker & Taylor, 86
Barcode, 73
Best Efforts, 33
Best Seller, 81
Bestselling, 111–112, 124, 132, 142, 179
Beta Readers, 98, 235
Big Five, 41, 71
Bio, 97, 104, 171, 211
Blog, 67, 81, 108, 112, 115, 117, 123, 142, 190, 192–193, 196, 198, 202, 207, 210, 216–219, 222–223, 235
  Blog Post, 202, 207, 210, 235
  Blog Tour, 112, 216–219, 222–223
  Blogger, 66, 183, 189, 197, 228
Book Community, 183
Book Marketing, 78, 94, 111–112, 114, 116, 118, 223
Book Printing Technology, 86
Book Production, 67, 83–84
Book Promotion, 185
Book Proposal, 95, 132, 172
Book Sales, 86, 112, 119, 216, 226
Book World, 131, 190, 199
BookBub, 118, 186–187, 190, 204, 218
Bookish, 209, 222, 224
Bookstagram, 192, 222
  Bookstagrammer, 189, 197, 228
Bookstore, 70, 151, 186, 207–208
Booksweeps, 186
BookTokker, 189
BookTube, 191
Bowker, 104
Brand, 24, 111, 119, 133, 171, 192, 223
Brick-and-Mortar, 71, 191

Budget, 48, 79, 180, 191–192, 223
Buoyancy, 131–132
Business Mindset, 24
Business Relationship, 31, 60
Buzzworthy, 227

C

Call to Action, 144
Canva, 117
Caray, Harry, 137
Career, 24–25, 32, 40, 51, 57, 79, 81, 84, 87, 116, 121–122, 124, 126, 185, 222, 226, 232, 234
Categories, 51, 70, 108
Character Development, 165
Chicago Cubs, 137
Chicago Manual of Style, 143
Children's Book Insider, 69
China, 150
Christian Fiction Readers Retreat, 225
Christian Writer's Manual of Style, 143
Christmas, 187
Cliché, 160
Client, 25, 31–32, 40, 45–46, 48, 56, 62, 137
Coach, 67, 97
Coachable, 149, 153
Collaboration, 36
Commission, 32
Communication, 45–46, 59, 104, 146, 194
Community, 78, 112–113, 151, 183, 185, 202, 222–226, 228–229, 232, 235–236
Comparable, 94, 96, 222
Competition, 67, 173
Concept, 94
Conciseness, 132
Conference, 96, 129–130, 141–142, 149–151, 183, 234
Conflict, 164
Content Edit, 41, 105
  Content Editor, 105, 155–156, 158–160, 162–164, 166–168
Content Marketing, 114
Contests, 108, 132
Contract, 26, 29–34, 38, 40, 42, 47, 54, 58, 60, 80, 89–90, 99–101, 104, 108, 121, 151, 178–179
  Contract Clauses, 34
  Contract Negotiations, 38
ConvertKit, 116

Copy Edit, 105–106
  Copy Editor, 169–170, 172, 174
Corrections, 107
Cover Design, 73–75, 104, 107, 109, 123, 207–208
Cover Letter, 94, 96
Craft of Writing, 66, 122, 132
Credentials, 78, 97, 128, 170
Critique Group, 41, 132, 178
Critique Partners, 98, 210
Customer Relationship Management, 104
Customer Service, 85

D

Debut Author, 123
  Debut Novel, 210
Description, 97, 108, 151, 171–172, 198
Design, 73–75, 104, 106–107, 109, 123, 193, 207–209, 212–213
Developmental Edit, 105, 155
  Developmental Editor, 105, 109, 150, 168
Dialogue, 156, 161–165, 194
Digital Distribution, 106
Discouragement, 234
Dissociative Disorders, 145
Distribution, 74–75, 83–84, 86, 106, 108
DIY, 209
Dr. Seuss, 236
Draft, 53, 100, 138, 166
Dream Publisher, 41
Dream Sequence, 160
Dual Time Periods, 162
Dykes, Amanda, 184

E

eBook, 104, 106–107, 118, 191–192
Editing, 32, 38, 40, 66–67, 73–75, 86, 103, 105–106, 138–139, 143, 169, 174, 178–179, 209
  Editing Phase, 179
Editorial Calendar, 98
Elevator Pitch, 127, 172
Email, 38–39, 45–46, 48, 53, 60, 72, 78–79, 81, 85, 89, 97, 99–100, 108, 112–119, 124–125, 128–129, 132, 170–171, 187, 191, 204
  Email List, 79, 112–115, 117–119, 187, 204
  Email Marketing, 112, 115, 117, 204
Emotional Response, 132

INDEX

Endorsements, 204–205
Engage, 186, 204, 223
   Engagement, 185–188, 217, 221–224, 226
   Engaging, 224, 226
English, 122, 137, 147, 177–178
Ethical, 30, 32
Expectations, 27, 34–36, 38, 40, 42, 45, 48–49, 121, 125, 220
Extrovert, 143

F

Facebook, 104, 115, 123, 185–186, 196, 203, 218, 222
Fanbase, 142–143, 172
Faulkner, William, 132
Feedback, 38, 46, 52, 122, 132, 152, 178, 205, 213, 225
Fiction, 225
Finding Readers, 184
First Impression, 207–208, 210, 212
First Line Friday, 190
First Person, 156, 211
First Read, 105
Flashback, 159–160
Fleshed-out Characters, 145
Font, 107, 132–133, 170, 208, 217
Ford, Harrison, 185
Format, 96, 106, 118, 132–133, 158, 169–170
   Formatted Galley, 107
   Formatting, 73–75, 80, 106–107, 169, 174
Franklin, Aretha, 231
Freebie, 186
Freelance Editing, 32
   Freelance Editor, 79, 132
Full, 25–26, 37, 41, 46, 52, 55, 70–71, 79–80, 94–96, 98, 115, 145, 150, 191, 199, 203, 225, 230
   Full Manuscript, 37, 41, 70, 80, 94–96

G

Gameplan, 117
Gap between Representation, 31
Gatekeeper, 62, 141, 147, 151
Gateways to Publication, 180
Genre, 24, 37, 39, 78–79, 90–91, 94, 96, 98, 122, 142, 164, 173, 184, 186–187, 195–196, 198–199, 208, 213, 222, 229
   Genre-jump, 24

Ghostwriter, 150
Goal of Marketing, 113
God, 68, 207, 210, 223, 225, 228, 234–236
GoodReads, 186, 190, 218
Grammar, 98, 106, 132, 151, 169, 174
Grant of Rights, 99
Graphic Design, 193
   Graphic Designer, 66–67
Guide, 73, 128, 143, 165
Guidelines, 48, 54–56, 78, 80, 94–96, 123, 128–130, 141, 197, 219

H

Happily Ever After, 233–234
Hard Edit, 100
Hard Work, 27, 62, 93, 139, 178, 180, 199, 226
Hardcover, 104, 106–107
Head Hopping, 157
Headshot, 104, 171, 197, 211
Hemingway, Ernest, 180
Hook, 96, 158, 162, 168, 170, 209, 212, 226
Hot New Releases, 90
Hyatt, Michael, 112
Hybrid Publishing, 74, 149, 151, 179

I

Imprint, 71, 75
Independent Book Publishers Association, 75
Independent Publishing, 73
Industry, 29, 32–33, 37–39, 42, 46, 53, 55–56, 58, 67–69, 71, 74–75, 79, 85, 90, 100, 122, 124–125, 127, 129, 139, 143, 145, 149–151, 153, 183–184, 187, 192–194, 203, 232–233
   Industry Roles, 42
   Industry Standards, 75, 100
Information Dump, 160
Ingram, 86
   IngramSpark, 107
Instagram, 46, 185–186, 190, 193, 195, 197–198, 230
Interior Layout, 66, 74–75, 107
International Standard Book Number, 104
   ISBN, 73, 104, 108
Internet, 26, 94–95, 128, 142, 178, 231
Internet Presence, 94
Interview, 24, 26, 132, 190

Introvert, 143

J
Jesus, 57, 234–235
JustRead, 219

K
Keywords, 108
Kindle Direct Publishing, 65–66
    KDP, 66
Kindle Edition, 118
Kindness, 53, 56, 61

L
Lag and Lull, 167
Language Acquisition, 137, 146–147
Lead Capture System, 116
    Lead Magnet, 116–117
Legal Advice, 30, 99
Libraries, 71, 86, 185
    Library, 105, 138, 143, 158, 183, 186
Library of Congress, 105
    LCCN, 105
Line Edit, 105–106, 109, 174
    Line Editor, 150, 169–171, 174–175
List-building, 115, 117
Literary Agent, 32, 41, 71

M
MailerLite, 116
Manuscript Delivery, 99
Manuscript Submission Checklist, 100
Market Guide, 128, 143
Market Research, 37, 39
Marketable, 77, 81
Marketing, 32, 41, 67, 69, 72, 74–75, 78, 85, 87, 89–90, 94, 107, 111–119, 172–173, 183, 185, 191, 194–195, 198, 204, 213, 215, 217–220, 223–224
    Marketing Potential, 89–90, 172
    Marketing Strategy, 204
    Marketing Tool, 115, 194–195, 218
    Marketing Toolbox, 111, 119
Marketing Sherpa, 115
Master of Firsts, 155–159, 168
Master of Lasts, 159
Media Kit, 197, 213, 218
Mentor, 72–73, 173

Metadata, 107
Microsoft Word, 80, 106
Midlist, 70
Midsize Publisher, 71
Mindset, 24, 137
Ministry, 127
Money, 24, 32, 70, 72, 74, 78, 81, 94, 121, 126–127, 185, 204, 208–209
Multi-published, 124, 132, 201
Murphy, Cecil, 150

N
Narrator, 157, 162
National Days, 224
Negotiate, 31–32, 99, 101
Network, 37–38, 41–42, 52, 67, 203, 216, 232
Newsletter, 81, 116–118, 123, 186, 198, 204, 212–213
Novel, 90, 155, 210
    Novelist, 158, 183
    Novella, 187
NY Times Bestseller, 179

O
Official Acceptance, 99
Onboarding Sequence, 116–117
Once Upon a Time, 233
One Sheet, 127, 171, 175
Online Community, 112–113
Online Presence, 78
Opting In, 117
Ormond, Julia, 185
Out of Print, 100

P
Pacing, 138, 146, 165
Paid Critique, 79
Paperback, 104, 106–107
Partnership, 36, 39, 108
Passive, 167–168
Patience, 54, 59, 97, 109, 197, 200
Pen Name, 170–171, 173
Permission-based, 117
Persistence, 98, 180
Pitch, 31, 127–128, 146, 172
Placing, 38, 162
Platform, 27, 41, 43, 66–67, 78–81, 84, 94–96, 98, 101, 107, 112, 115, 117–118,

122–123, 126, 142–143, 173, 186, 188, 190–191, 193, 203, 215, 218, 225
Plot, 105, 155, 165, 168, 192, 209, 231
Poetry, 152
Point of View, 156–158
    POV, 156–158, 163–164, 179
Policies, 55, 104, 123, 197, 199
Polish, 33, 90, 98
Pre-order Alert, 118
Pre-publication, 103
Print Run, 66, 71, 107
Product, 24, 83, 106, 117, 208, 215, 219
Professionalism, 27, 31, 48, 53, 56, 78, 121, 124–125, 132–133, 207
Project Management System, 86, 103
Project Manager, 72, 83
Prologue, 158, 162
Promotion, 83, 85, 108, 185–187, 215
Promotional Copies, 108
Proofreader, 150, 174
Proposal, 33, 47, 52–53, 55, 77–80, 90, 94–98, 100, 118, 124, 128–129, 132–133, 170, 172, 175
Prospect, 24, 80
Protagonist, 96, 162, 165–166
Publication, 65, 67, 75, 89–90, 98–99, 103, 108, 131, 133, 139, 141, 145, 149–151, 158–159, 178–180
    Publication Process, 65
    Publication Slots, 99
Publication Board, 150–151
    Pub Board, 55, 97, 151–152, 172
Publicist, 112, 128
    Publicity Tour, 183, 207, 216, 218, 220, 223
Publishable, 100
Published, 39, 65–67, 69, 74, 78–79, 81, 90, 93–95, 98–99, 107, 112–113, 118, 122, 124, 127, 129, 132, 139, 143, 173, 178–179, 191, 201, 209–210, 236
Publishing Contract, 32, 89–90
Publishing House, 42, 53, 56, 65, 72–74, 95, 98, 103, 123–125, 133, 141, 143, 147, 150–151, 155, 168, 170, 178, 235
Publishing Industry, 37, 67, 71, 85, 90, 122, 124–125, 127, 129, 139, 143, 145, 149–151, 153, 184, 194, 232–233
Publishing Predators, 73
Publishing Process, 72, 74, 83–84, 103–104, 106, 108, 123

Publishing Professional, 84
Punctuation, 106

Q

Query, 27, 38–39, 55, 65, 80, 96–97, 128, 170, 175
    Querying, 27, 38, 40, 61–62
Quiller-Couch, Sir Arthur, 132

R

Reading Fee, 73
ReadingIsMySuperPower, 183, 190
Recently Published Works, 39
Reddit, 185–186
Rejection, 49, 90, 124, 151, 234
Relationship, 24, 30–31, 36, 39, 53, 56–61, 104, 143, 146, 156–157, 163–165, 179, 196, 205, 222
Release, 80, 103–104, 113, 118, 187, 196, 212, 217–218, 220, 231
Representation, 27, 31, 40
Reputation, 39, 55, 58, 72, 74–75
Research, 27, 37, 39–40, 43, 51, 76–77, 93–94, 98, 101, 108, 116, 123, 128, 130, 132–133, 141–142, 165–166, 199, 202, 208
Resource, 77, 81, 143
Respect, 45–46, 49, 53, 125, 196–197, 199, 217, 228
Returns, 234
Reversion of Rights, 100
Reviewer, 183–184, 189, 199, 205, 221, 228–230
    Reviews, 90, 97–98, 112, 190, 195, 198–199, 203–204, 222, 230, 232
Revise, 100
    Revisions, 33, 38, 47, 105, 109
Rights, 30, 32–33, 68, 75, 99–100, 123
Rodgers & Hammerstein, 224
Rough Draft, 138
Royalties, 32, 70–71, 83, 99, 149
    Royalty Statements, 85
Ruchti, Cynthia, 234

S

Sales Potential, 83
Sales Reports, 85, 104
Sample Chapters, 55, 96, 100, 174
Scam, 74

INDEX

Scene, 58, 80, 105, 109, 152, 156–157, 160–161, 165–166
Screenwriter, 150, 158
Second Person, 156
Seekerville, 202
Self-editing, 66, 174
Self-publish, 66, 90–91, 121, 149
    Self-publishing, 59, 66, 73–75
    Self-publishing Assistance, 74
Sendinblue, 116
Sentence Structure, 164, 169, 174
Series, 96, 116, 159, 191
Service Providers, 73–74
Shiny Object, 122
Sign Language, 177
Signup Form, 116
Simultaneous Storylines, 162
Simultaneous Submissions, 141
Single Submission, 25
Skillset, 143
Slush Pile, 61, 97
Small Press, 59, 72, 74, 77, 85, 99, 127, 129
Smiley, Jane, 183
Social Media, 31, 45, 54, 66, 78–79, 81, 108, 111–115, 117, 119, 123, 125, 142, 155, 179, 186–188, 190, 193, 195, 197–198, 202–205, 212–213, 215–219, 222, 224, 228–229
    Social Media Marketing, 113–114
    Social Media Tour, 216–219
Social Triggers, 113
Spell-checker, 169
Spelling, 106, 169, 174
Stand-alone, 159
Standard Contract, 99–101
Standard Manuscript Formatting, 80
Story Arc, 144, 148, 151, 158
Storytelling, 132
Street Team, 98, 223
Structure, 105, 117, 158, 164, 169, 174, 194
Style, 45, 143, 208
Submissions, 25, 38, 41, 45–46, 48–49, 51–54, 56, 61, 71, 75, 85, 93–94, 96–97, 104, 123, 128–130, 141, 147, 151, 172
    Submissions Guidelines, 54, 94, 96, 123
    Submissions Process, 56
    Submissions Strategies, 38, 49, 51–52, 54, 56
Subplot, 105
Subscribers, 113–114, 118, 186–187

Subsidiary Rights, 99
Success, 36, 78, 97, 112, 199
Supplementary Services, 32
Synopsis, 96, 171–173
Syntax, 105

T

Tagline, 170
Takeaways, 61, 196, 205
Talent, 97, 132, 150
Target Audience, 97, 113–114
Team Player, 124–125
Teamwork, 186–187
Technical Writer, 152
Television, 81, 187
    TV, 35, 137
Termination Clause, 30–31, 60
Territory, 99
The Call, 24–27, 37, 45, 99, 144
Third Person, 157, 211
TikTok, 185–186, 190–191
Tolkien, JRR, 180
Top Ten Tuesday, 190
Track Record, 27, 99–101
Trade, 70
Traditional Publishing, 65–67, 69–70, 73, 75, 78, 89, 103, 108, 149, 151
    Traditional Publishing House, 65, 73
Transitions, 164, 166
Trends, 39, 42, 46, 68, 90, 208, 213
Trope, 209
Tutorial Videos, 116
Twitter, 115, 185–186, 195

U

Unagented Submissions, 71
Unethical, 30, 32, 54
Unsolicited Manuscript
    Unsolicited Submissions, 128
Usage, 106, 132

V

Vanity Press, 72–73
    Vanity Publishing, 72, 74
Vellum, 106
Viewpoint, 156
Virtual Conference, 129–130
Visibility, 95, 122–123, 126

Vision, 67, 75, 137, 141
Vlog, 142
Voiceovers, 191

W

Website, 32, 66–68, 72, 75, 78–79, 81, 94–95, 97, 104, 115–118, 123–124, 128–129, 190, 197, 207, 210–213
Website Submissions, 128
Whac-A-Mole, 185
Wholesaler, 86
Widget, 116
Word Count, 96, 100, 155
Word of Mouth, 202–205
Write What You Know, 78
Writer, 42, 97, 122, 132, 138, 142–143, 150, 152, 178, 235
Writing Career, 79, 81, 122, 232
Writing Craft, 84
    Writing Skills, 122, 132, 152
Writing Library, 143

Z

Zoom, 95, 123–124, 129

Made in the USA
Monee, IL
24 October 2022

6c9aa47b-3560-48ed-b871-fa7b549b2adbR01